יִתְגַּדֵל וְיִתְקַדֵּשׁ שְׁמֵהּ רַבָּא, בְּעָלְמָא דִּי־
בְרָא כִרְעוּתֵהּ, וְיַמְלִיךְ מַלְכוּתֵהּ בְּחַיֵּיכוֹן
וּבְיוֹמֵיכוֹן וּבְחַיֵּי דְכָל־בֵּית־יִשְׂרָאֵל, בַּעֲגָלָא
וּבִזְמַן קָרִיב. וְאִמְרוּ אָמֵן:

יְהֵא שְׁמֵהּ רַבָּא מְבָרַךְ, לְעָלַם וּלְעָלְמֵי עָלְמַיָּא.

יִתְבָּרַךְ וְיִשְׁתַּבַּח וְיִתְפָּאַר וְיִתְרֹמַם וְיִתְנַשֵּׂא
וְיִתְהַדָּר וְיִתְעַלֶּה וְיִתְהַלָּל שְׁמֵהּ דְּקֻדְשָׁא.
בְּרִיךְ הוּא לְעֵלָּא (*וּלְעֵלָּא) מִן־כָּל־בִּרְכָתָא
וְשִׁירָתָא, תֻּשְׁבְּחָתָא וְנֶחֱמָתָא, דַּאֲמִירָן
בְּעָלְמָא. וְאִמְרוּ אָמֵן:

יְהֵא שְׁלָמָא רַבָּא מִן־שְׁמַיָּא וְחַיִּים, עָלֵינוּ
וְעַל־כָּל־יִשְׂרָאֵל. וְאִמְרוּ אָמֵן:

עֹשֶׂה שָׁלוֹם בִּמְרוֹמָיו, הוּא יַעֲשֶׂה שָׁלוֹם
עָלֵינוּ וְעַל־כָּל־יִשְׂרָאֵל. וְאִמְרוּ אָמֵן:

OLD BOHEMIAN AND MORAVIAN JEWISH CEMETERIES

· PASEKA ·

STARÉ MĚSTO POD LANDŠTEJNEM

OLD BOHEMIAN AND MORAVIAN

JEWISH CEMETERIES

PASEKA
PRAGUE
1991

Petr Ehl
Arno Pařík
Jiří Fiedler

KYNŠPERK NAD OHŘÍ

GARDENS
OF LIFE

In the territories of Bohemia and Moravia, in the course of the last thousand years, over 600 Jewish religious communities and prayer societies came into being. As a consequence of dramatic historical events, however, many of them ceased to exist—some as early as the Middle Ages, others as late as the turn of this century, when a mass exodus of inhabitants took place from small rural communities to larger towns and emerging industrial centres. For the majority of historical Jewish communities, however, the ultimate doom was spelled by the Holocaust, during which Czech and Moravian Jews were deported by the Nazis to concentration and extermination camps, where close to ninety per cent of them perished. The only relics of these once important Jewish communities, which can still be found in many small towns and villages in Bohemia and Moravia, are the dilapidated remnants of former ghettos, neglected synagogues and weed-ridden cemeteries. Of the latter quite a few were preserved, evidently because they were the least suited for practical purposes.

In spite of the fact that Jews settled in Bohemia and Moravia as early as the 10th century, with the only exception of Prague, none of the medieval Jewish cemeteries situated within the town walls or in their close proximity have lasted to this day. These cemeteries were ruined during the numerous medieval pogroms, or else the tombstones were used as building material after the expulsion of Jewish inhabitants from towns. In con-

5

ŠVIHOV

nection with the Crusades, throughout the 12th century, Jewish cemeteries were devastated in Central Europe of which evidence is given in many Papal bulls which advocated their protection. Explicit prohibition against desecrating Jewish cemeteries, a capital offence implying confiscation of all property, was only later included in the Jewish privileges, which were issued by Přemysl Otakar II for Jewish communities in 1254. The oldest known Jewish tombstones in Bohemia and Moravia, usually discovered during the demolition of old town walls or during construction work for the spreading towns in the last century, date from the 13th and 14th centuries. Other Jewish cemeteries were ruined in numerous pogroms in the middle of the 14th century, during the Hussite wars and in particular following the expulsion of Jews from Silesian and Moravian Royal towns in the years 1453 and 1454. Likewise in Bohemia, at the end of the 15th century and in the first half of the 16th century attempts were made to drive out Jews from many towns, which culminated in the double expulsion from Prague and from the whole country during the reign of Ferdinand I in the years 1541 and 1557. That is why the oldest Jewish tombstones which have been preserved in their original places date from the 15th century and can only be found at old Jewish cemeteries in Prague and Kolín. Tombstones from the 16th century are also very rare and apart from the two mentioned towns can only be found at cemeteries in Brandýs nad Labem, Mladá Boleslav, Libochovice, Stráž, and also in Moravia's Ivančice. Tombstones dating from the 17th and 18th centuries are present in many urban and rural cemeteries and due to their significant numbers allow us to examine their evolution and local peculiarities. Tombstones preserved at a Jewish cemetery, however, are usually far more recent than the cemetery itself, as the oldest tombstones were either destroyed during a temporary expulsion, or were uprooted and sank into the soil by their own weight. Undoubtedly, wooden monuments, the lifespan of which was far shorter and which fell to ruin through weathering over a few decades, were routinely used in rural cemeteries in the past.

Tradition and religious custom have always called upon the Jews to hold in exceptional respect the resting places of their predecessors. In Hebrew a cemetery is called *bet kewarot*—the house or the place of graves (Neh. 2:3), but more commonly *bet ha-Chajim*—the house or garden of life, or *bet olam*—the house of eternity (Eccl. 12:5). In other words, names which in a sense express the belief in the transcendence of human life, although the Old Testament and Judaism, unlike other religions, do not deny human mortality.

Any act at odds with respect for the dead is prohibited in a cemetery, and its territory and facilities are banned from being used for other purposes. According to Jewish law, as described in the Talmud, the dead are to be guaranteed the eternal inviolability of their graves. A number of consequences derive from this religious principle which until today determine the particular appearance and atmosphere of Jewish cemeteries. This principle is also the reason why so many Jewish cemeteries and old tombstones have been preserved to this day, whilst in much older Christian cemeteries, where after some time graves are abolished, we can usually only find tombstones dating from the last century.

On the basis of a religious ruling to provide for the inviolability of their ancestors' graves, the Jews when founding cemeteries tried to purchase the sites from the owners or from the towns on a permanent basis. For this privilege they had at times to pay considerable sums, in exchange for which they received inferior sites unsuitable for any other purpose. It is for this reason that we often encounter old Jewish cemeteries on steep hillsides or in wooded hilly country, on tops of hills or on the slopes of rivers, brooks and valleys, on sites located at a considerable distance from the respective town or village or otherwise accessible only with difficulty. It is due to this choice of remote and concealed places for establishing cemeteries that a relatively large number of them have been preserved to this day. More often, however, the establishment of a cemetery under the conditions of permanent ownership was rejected by the town or community and the Jews were compelled—particularly in the early periods—to transport their dead to cemeteries situated at a considerable distance. Although Jewish communities tried for understandable reasons to secure their own burial grounds as soon as possible, its establishment usually took place when conditions were more favourable and was dated later than the original Jewish settlement in a given community. To protect the graves from desecration and damage, the cemeteries were surrounded by a tall stone wall and a gate (often double) in the form of a small house which in small rural cemeteries also served as a mortuary.

In Jewish communities, all the religious and practical aspects connected with harbouring the sick and the dying, the funeral itself and comfort for the bereaved has for centuries been under the care of a society known as *Hevra Kaddishah* the holy or burial brotherhood. The brotherhood served all members of the community on equal terms as the duty to care for the sick and the dying and their funeral is considered one of the most important religious rulings. Its origin is based on the principle that no individual is to derive material benefit from the death of another, while through the intermediary of the burial brotherhood any profits serve the community as a whole. The oldest known burial brotherhood was founded in 1564 in Prague by Rabbi Eliezer Ashkenazy, and later this important social institution was etablished in most Jewish communities in Bohemia and Moravia. It frequently even preceded the founding of independent religious communities and formed their basis. Membership in the fraternity is open to senior married men of integrity. Their task is to visit and care for the sick and to comfort relatives and see to it that the patient is

surrounded by the *minyan* (a gathering of ten men indispensable for divine service), who recite to the dying until his ultimate decease prayers and at the moment of death also *Shema Yisrael*—the Jewish profession of faith.

The funeral itself should take place without delay, if possible on the very day of death (Deut. 21:23), with the exception of the Sabbath, the Day

VELKÁ BUKOVINA

of Atonement and the first day of major festivals. After death the body of the deceased is carried by the accompanying members of the burial brotherhood to the *bet taharah*—the house of purification, which was frequently to be found directly in the cemetery or in its vicinity at the edge of the ghetto. Here, while prayers and psalms are read, the ceremony of cleansing the body with lukewarm water is carried out, the basis of which is considered to be the biblical quotation „As naked he camme forth, so naked shall he return . . . (Eccl. 5:15)—man is washed when he is born and should be washed when he dies. This ceremony may even be performed on the Sabbath. Subsequently, the body is clothed in a shroud of pure linen, men are in addition dressed in a *tallit*—a

prayer shawl, and laid in a simple wooden coffin free of ornaments, emphasizing the equality of all at death. As it has always been the wish of pious Jews to be buried in the land of the ancestors, tradition has it to place under the head of the deceased a small pouch filled with some Palestine soil or at least to dust his face with this soil. Should burial not be possible on the day of death, the body would be deposited in the mortuary at the cemetery, where members of the funereal fraternity would hold a wake over the deceased until the day of the funeral.

Accompanying the deceased and partaking in the funeral is also considered a religious duty— *hesed shel emet*, even justifying the interruption of the study of the Torah. Originally the seven pauses in the funeral procession on the way to the grave corresponded to the seven grammatical forms of the word *hevel* (death, transience), the seven days of creation and the seven stages of life. During the pauses prayers are read as well as Psalms 16 or 91. In rural areas the ancient tradition long survived that on leaving the cemetery the procession threw over their backs, towards the grave, grass and soil as a sign of transience, saying „Remember that we are of dust." On leaving the cemetery after the funeral rites the participants symbolically wash their hands at the water pump or in a vessel known as a *kiyor*, installed for this purpose at the entrance to the cemetery.

A week of mourning follows the funeral, *shivah*—seven days, when it is a duty to visit the bereaved and comfort them. In the house of mourning prayers are said on seven consecutive days. The mourners refrain from attending any social events and celebrations, and from working or studying religious scripts. They just pray, sitting on the floor or on low stools as a sign of grief (this is the origin of the phrase „to sit *shivah*"). After the funeral of close relatives the mourning period is 30 days—the month of mourning. After the death of a parent the mourning lasts for 11 months—the year of mourning. On the first anniversary of the parent's funeral, and on subsequent anniversaries of the death, the bereaved devote the day to visiting the cemetery, praying and lighting a memorial lamp known as *Yahrzeit*. The anniversary of the death of a parent is a day of reminiscence of the deceased. Graves and cemeteries are usually visited on the anniversary of the death of parents or prominent teachers, on *Rosh Ha-Shanah* (New Year's Day), on fast-days or days of mourning, traditionally the *9th of Av*—the anniversary of the destruction of the first and second Jerusalem Temple, or the *7th of Adar*, which is considered to be the anniversary of Moses' death. Likewise, in times of persecution and expulsion, members of the community gathered for the last time at the cemetery to bid farewell to the graves of their parents, the most precious possession they had to leave behind. According to early tradition the Jews on visiting the grave of a loved one or a prominent figure deposit on the tombstone a small pebble as a token of remembrance, allegedly on the basis of the duty of wayfarers in antiquity to add a stone on the grave-mounds of the dead in the desert.

By the first anniversary of the funeral the head of the grave should already be provided with a tombstone, the completion of which often required considerable time. The Talmudic command of inviolability of graves says that at least six palms of soil should divide individual graves. Because of the usual lack of space and also to avoid inadvertent violation of old graves, the dead in old Jewish cemeteries were buried without any distinction, according to the sequence of the funerals, in lines side by side. Only temporarily could a space be reserved for close family members, but on the other hand, persons who lived in mutual conflict or hostility, were if possible buried separated from one another. Similarly, impious persons were not buried beside the just. In some important cemeteries, a special place was reserved in the so-called row of honour for rabbis and prominent teachers, men of exceptional religious

9

faith or those who in some other way earned merit in the community. In this row, the largest and most richly decorated tombstones are usually found today.

To avoid defiling the biblical priestly tribe of *Kohen*, their descendants were not allowed to enter the cemetery (Lev. 21:1—4). But to allow them to visit the graves of their close relatives without having to walk across the cemetery, some cemeteries provide special rows near the wall opposite the entrance for the graves of descendants of the Kohen family. These are accessible through little gates in the nearby wall called Kohen gates.

Similarly, in some places special rows of graves were reserved for members of the biblical family of *Levites*, the temple assistants, although they were not banned from entering a cemetery. In large cemeteries a special place known as *nefele* was sometimes reserved for the burial of children. Also buried in cemeteries with all honour are the parchment Torah scrolls damaged during violent pogroms, natural catastrophes or worn by time and therefore withdrawn from use.

An obvious result of the command of inviolability of all graves was that even in a cemetery of a small community the area became completely full as time passed, and the cemetery had to be enlarged. Many old cemeteries were thus enlarged several times through the purchase of new sites, if possible immediately adjacent to the old cemetery, and again protected by a common wall. These extensions took place in particular in the second half of the 19th century following the lifting of restrictive laws in the period of the greatest upsurge in the population of Jewish communities. Thus added to old cemeteries, established on inaccessible slopes, were new purchases of extensive lots of land more favourably positioned either above the existing location, as is the case at Třebíč, Jindřichův Hradec and Rakovník, or in the close vicinity, as can be seen in Mikulov, Uherský Brod and Brtnice. Most often, however, in the second half of the 19th century, when the enlargement of old cemeteries proved impossible due to unfavourable location, cemeteries were founded on new and more easily accessible locations or right in the neighbourhood of urban cemeteries, as is the case in Prague, Roudnice, Pardubice, Prostějov and elsewhere. That is the reason why many Jewish communities which stayed uninterruptedly for several centuries in one location, often have two or even three cemeteries. One reason for founding new cemeteries in the last century was the building expansion of communities which necessitated the abolition of old cemeteries. Some of the most important tombstones were pi-

ously transferred to the new cemetery. These were then accorded a special place or set into the wall of the cemetery.

In the more distant past another solution was indispensable when cemeteries were filled to capacity and could not be enlarged, and new ones could not be founded. Old graves were covered with a thick layer of new soil to accommodate the deceased. The tombstones of old graves were then transferred to the new layer of graves and were set alongside the new stones. Such places are conspicuous today by the dense accumulation of stelae dating from various periods, as is characteristic of the chronically cramped Old Jewish Cemetery in Prague. Old tombstones were also removed from the soil and piled at the edge of the cemetery to form terrace-like walls on the sloping plot of land, as is the case in Mikulov. More frequently, however, the tombstones were laid flat on the old grave for protection and covered with a new layer of earth. As time passed this became the natural fate of most of the oldest tombstones which fell and sunk into the soil to disappear either by their own weight or as a result of damage. Only since the end of the last century have the oldest tombstones, the original location of which is no longer certain, been transferred to special places near the wall of the cemetery or implanted directly in the wall.

A Jewish tombstone, in Hebrew called a *mazzevah*, has a religious purpose, to protect a burial place from disturbance and to mark it and to preserve the name of the deceased. It also has considerable historical significance. Since the early Middle Ages the principal and often the only decoration on the tombstone is an inscription in Hebrew, always giving the name of the deceased, the date of death or of the funeral, but also various eulogies, which may contain interesting facts about the profession and life of the deceased. The historical significance of the epitaph as a written source for the history of the Jews depends mainly on the age of the tombstone. Due to the fact that

knowledge about early Jewish settlements is scarce, an inscription on a tombstone may be the only and irreplaceable evidence of the existence of a Jewish community in a given place and time. Tombstones dated before Thirty Years' War which outside the Old Jewish Cemetery in Prague have only been preserved in very small numbers, are extremely rare. More recent tombstones from the 18th and 19th centuries are far less historically significant because other written records exist from this period. Of course, tombstones from this period pertaining to prominent figures, which are usually more detailed and which acquaint us with precious data about the life and work of the deceased, are of special historical importance.
ical importance.

From the earliest preserved medieval examples onwards, inscriptions on Jewish tombstones are written in the Hebrew quadratic alphabet with forms which became stabilized in antiquity. This alphabet with its repeated quadratic form of letters and graded thickness of vertical and oblique strokes offers many opportunities for ornamental artistic stylization. This was incidentally also fully applied in medieval Hebrew manuscripts. The writing of the oldest medieval tombstones in our territory is relatively large and not regularly placed. In the Renaissance however, smaller regular types of letters were used, sharply cut in deep basrelief and very legible thanks to the outstanding shading. In the Baroque period, Hebrew quadratic script assumed larger dimensions and decorative forms cut in shallow basrelief on a roughened background became more common. The execution of this kind of writing, with its basic rectangular shape and the pronounced strokes of the upper baseline, always maintains a balanced composition of the inscription in the surface of the tombstone as well as sufficient space for making the most of the particular features of each letter.

For the historical appreciation of an inscription, the date is the most important item of information. As Hebrew has no special characters for numbers, it expresses numerical values by means of letters according to their sequence in the alphabet. The date usually gives the day in the week, the day in the month and the year according to the Jewish era „from the creation of the world", which precedes the Christian era by 3760 years. In other words, the date of all our known tombstones falls into the sixth millennium. The year is not always expressed by a sequence of letters in the conventional way but by means of a chronogram, i. e. the addition of numerical values to letters or words made specially conspicuous within the text of the epitaph.

The heading or the beginning of the inscription usually indicates the personal name of the deceased, made more specific by a patronymic, and in the case of women also the name of her husband. Men's names are usually marked with the relationship to the family of the Kohens or to the Levites, a distinguished person of this origin is described as *Kohen Zedek*, priest of justice, or *Segan Leviyim*, Levite prince. Inscriptions on the most ancient tombstones rarely bear an established family name. Only since the 16th century has the name of the community or country of origin been often added to personal names. A number of well-known Jewish family names, such as Hořovský, Brandejs, Tausk, Kolín, Pardubic, Lieben, Roudnic, Náchod or Poděbrad were derived from names of Bohemian towns. Other common family names, such as Polak, Moravec, Ungar, Schlesinger or Sachs developed from the names of countries of origin. While male biblical names on tombstones remained the same for centuries, female names were subject to changes. Inscriptions even bear folk names, describing good characteristics, beautiful appearance or names based on flowers and birds.

Most names of the deceased and his father are supplemented by some kind of honorary title, the most frequent being *rabbi*—teacher, master, which later lost its original meaning and became a common courteous form of address. To revert to its original meaning, the term was used in its emphatic form, abbreviated as MHRR, *Morenu ha-rab rabbi*, rabbi our master, our teacher. This title was only given to persons performing the office of rabbi or *dayyan*—judge, while the supreme rabbi was designated with the title *av bet-din*—father of the rabbi's court. On some occasions, in the case of exceptionally learned rabbis, the honorary title *gaon* was added which used to be given to rectors of ancient Talmudic academies. The titles *alluf* and *katzin*— prince, were given to prominent representatives of the community, who were not necessarily scholars. To describe public offices in the community's administration the terms *gabbai* or *rosh*—a senior, and the very honorary title *parnas*, the chief administrative officer of a community were used. The lowest status is expressed by the term *shammash*—the sexton of a synagogue, who in the past, however, also had important duties. *Kadosh*—saint, was formerly used as the honorary title of martyrs, later it was used for all who died an unnatural death, which is considered something of a propitiatory sacrifice. In the case of women the sole title used was *marat*—married women, or exceptionally *rabbanit* in the case of a wife or daughter of a rabbi.

Added to the name of the deceased and in particular to that of his father are various eulogies—benedictions, among which the most repetitive was the traditional "cherished memory" or "the memory of the just is blessed" (Proverbs 10:7), expressed by the abbreviations ZL or ZCL, similarly as the quotation wishing a blessed posthumous life, used exclusively on tombstones since medieval times up to this day „Let his soul be bound in the bundle of life" (I. Sam. 25:29). Faith in the transience of human life are expressed in phrases like „he left for his world", „he was reunited with his people" or „his soul returned to its home", „he ascended to the heavenly heights", „he ascended to speak for his people" or „he joined scholars in heaven".

The largest part of an inscription, however, was

devoted to praising the character and deeds of the deceased. In men the most appreciated attributes are sincerity, justice, wisdom and eloquence, as well as mercy, generosity in charity, pious living („He walked along direct and proper paths"), learning („He sought learning incessantly and resolutely"), support of studies („His house was open to those who seek Learning"). Similarly, as with their names, the eulogies of women are more varied. Even here we most often encounter epithets connected with bravery, virtue, forthrightness, sincerity, justice, keen mind and wise heart. But beauty and kindness are also mentioned.

Reading Hebrew tombstone epitaphs is difficult not only due to the frequent illegibility of the inscriptions, but also because they often contain abbreviations and colloquial forms and phrases which are not always grammatically correct, though they do not lack a certain linguistic charm. The inscriptions on the oldest medieval tombstones are characterized by austere conciseness, and are usually limited to the most important particulars. Most interesting among them are undoubtedly the epitaphs of the 15th and 16th centuries, marked by considerable individualism and diversity of contents, while the more recent voluminous baroque texts lose the distinctiveness of the earlier inscriptions but show a marked effort for specific poetic expression. From the stylistic point of view, Hebrew epitaphs reveal the endeavour to lace the text with the greatest possible number of reminiscences and quotations from biblical literature, which in the new context often acquire a different meaning. This tendency is the basis of the so-called mosaic style, which was to flourish fully in the baroque period. The most interesting inscriptions use rhythmized prose which makes even the form of these texts more poetry-like.

Jewish tombstones, however, are also of considerable significance for history of Jewish art. In spite of the fact that the craftsmen were probably never exclusively Jewish, the composi-

tion and ornamentation was the result of close cooperation with the authors of the inscription and with other artisans from the ghetto, without whose participation the creation of the most valuable examples of Jewish funereal design would be unthinkable. These tombstones must therefore be considered one of the kinds of traditional Jewish art, which in all its aspects grew from specific cul-

RYCHNOV NAD KNĚŽNOU

tural and religious traditions. These allow us to examine the close connections between the ornamentation of Hebrew manuscripts and prints, synagogue textiles and jewellery, and that of the Jewish tombstones themselves to discover their common symbolic forms and the special language of signs, which over the centuries Jewish tradition created or adapted to its needs. Tombstones, in comparison with other forms of Jewish art, may seem to be less perfect, but they contain stronger evidence than any other form of art of the linkage between Jewish and local artistic traditions, which gives rise to diversity and originality of new designs.

The origin of the traditional Ashkenazic Jewish tombstone of the vertical type cannot be accurately determined for lack of examples preserved from the oldest period. In its development it is probably connected with the inscription plates from the Jewish catacombs of late antiquity and particularly with the rusticized design of provincial Roman tombstones and stelae. The oldest preserved tombstones of this type, dating from the 7th century onwards in southern Italy and France (Narbonne from the year 668, Brindisi from the year 832, Lyon from 1101), have the shape of an oblong or square plate with a carved Hebrew inscription. A larger number of medieval Ashkenazic tombstones dating from the 13th and 14th centuries was discovered in communities in France, the Rhineland and in Lower Austria, but they were preserved *in situ* only in the most ancient Central European Jewish cemeteries in Worms and Frankfurt. In Bohemia the oldest medieval tombstones dating from the 14th century were found in Prague and Cheb, in Moravia's Brno and Znojmo, the latter being the site of a tombstone dated 1256, which is the earliest known Jewish tombstone in the Czech lands. Of these oldest preserved examples it is evident that medieval Jewish tombstones had the form of roughly hewn oblong stone slabs, often not quite regular in form, topped rectangularly, with be-

velled angles, more rarely with a half-circle and quite exceptionally with the shape of a Gothic trefoil, usually without any ornamentation except for the relatively large carved letters of the Hebrew inscription and at times, a deep recess forming a frame around the inscription. The form of completing these simplest stelae determines the basic types of the Ashkenazic tombstone as it later developed in many modifications and variations until the middle of the 19th century.

Popular at the turn of the 14th and 15th centuries was the wider rectangular and even square shaped strictly right-angled type of tombstone with a projecting frieze on the upper side or a broadly framed inscription space. These tombstones were usually made of sandstone. The relatively thick and large slabs, only roughly finished on the reverse side, are effective by their simple block shape and their monumentality. Letters carved in deep basrelief are executed with precision, the end letters of a line are occasionally extended, as if in a manuscript, to obtain greater balance of the space. The oldest tombstones of this type are to be found at the cemetery in Worms (Germany). From 1439 onwards they also appear in Prague, where with slight modifications they were used until the end of 16th century. Prague tombstones of this type, with the strictly right-angled shape, balanced proportions and precision of the sharply carved letters constitute a specific style which is suitably complemented by the stylistic refinement and individuality of the inscriptions. In Bohemia, tombstones of this type can be encountered in a somewhat rougher form at Jewish cemeteries in Kolín, Brandýs nad Labem, Mladá Boleslav, Libochovice and Stráž, where the direct influence of the Prague examples may be presumed. A similar type is to be found in Moravia at the cemetery in Ivančice, and its more recent 17th century modification exists at cemeteries in Mikulov, Uherský Brod, Česká Lípa and Holešov.

In spite of evident conservatism and observance of past tradition and forms, during the second half of the 16th century the decoration of tombstones shows attempts at the more elaborate composition and decorative elements of the Renaissance. The right-angled form is disrupted by a low shield decorated with compressed volutes. The inscription is framed by a Renaissance cartouche or a hint of semicolumns in low relief along both sides, emphasizing segmentation of the inscription space into two or three fields. Together with this rather timid attempt at dividing the space, which interrupts the hitherto harsh compactness and heavy monumentality of slabs there is a change of material, too. In Prague, instead of the dark sandstone, Slivenec marble is increasingly used. This is remarkable for its pink-brown colouring and pronounced inner markings, which early in the 17th century clearly predominated at Prague's Old Jewish Cemetery. At that time the ornamentation shows ample use of Renaissance decorative elements. On this basis, a new system of architectural composition of the stele surface was gradually elaborated: the inscription area topped by a semi-circle is on either side framed by pilasters or half columns with a frieze or an entablature in which, situated in a cartouche, is the introductory inscription. The entire stele ends in a volute or cleaved shield with a central extension.

The development of this basic architectural composition of the tombstone space can be examined in many varieties throughout the 17th and 18th centuries in connection with the general development of style from late Renaissance through Baroque and Rococo to the period of Classicism, when the area of the tombstone is again integrated, marked plastic segmentation disappears and simplification leads to the basic type of semi-circular top of the stele which in various forms was continually preserved in rural cemeteries. Due to the influence of Italian Renaissance Hebrew prints, architectural composition asserted itself in all types of Jewish plastic art, at the end of the 16th century, leading its appearance towards greater diversity for at least the next two centuries. This development in the ornamentation of Jewish tombstones can be found in its most pronounced form at the Old Jewish Cemetery in Prague. Tombstones dating from the 17th and 18th centuries, however, are also represented in nearly half of all cemeteries in the Czech

15

and Moravian countryside. Here, however, the architectural type of composition is used less frequently and in a simplified form, elements of tectonic composition lose their function and are frequently used as independent decorative motifs.

Towards the end of the 16th century, apart from common ornamental Renaissance elements, tombstones in Prague bore for the first time plastic relief signs with symbolic meanings anchored in Jewish tradition—a grape, the symbol of wisdom and fertility, the crown of a good name, *Magen David*, the six-pointed Star of David, a money box as the symbol of charity, a pair of heraldic lions and others, which express common symbols of Judaism or the origin, name or occupation of the deceased. Blessing hands mark e.g. the

tombstones of the descendants of the biblical Kohen tribe of temple priests, the signs of a pitcher or a musical instrument mark the tombstones of their assistants from the Levite tribe. Personal or family names of the deceased are usually symbolized by relief signs of animals: a lion for the Hebrew name of *Yehudah* or *Aryeh*, in the colloquial form *Leb*, a deer for *Cvi* or *Hirsch*, a bear for *Dov* or *Beer*, a wolf for *Zeev* or *Wolf*, a polecat for *Iltis*, a goose for *Gans*, a cockerel for the family name of *Hahn*, a fox for the name of the *Fuchs* family, a carp sometimes for the family name *Karpeles*, a mouse for *Maysl* etc.

The occupation of the deceased was most often symbolized by relief of a tool characteristic for a certain occupation. Thus we find scissors on the graves of tailors, lancets in the case of doctors, mortars for chemists and violins for musicians. On the grave of a scholar, a reader of prayers or a bookbinder, one finds a book. Likewise, there may be a quill for a scribe, instruments for circumcision on the tombstone of a *mohel*, and a scroll of the Torah or a shelf with books on the tombstones of rabbis or scholars. Special features at the Prague cemetery are figural motifs to be found on certain tombstones — most frequently the figure of a woman on the tombstones of young, unmarried girls (also to be seen in Brandýs), the figures of Adam and Eve in paradise on the tombstone of a woman named Havah and the unusual representation of a woman spinning *zizith* — the tassels of a prayer garment. Quite unique is the image of the supreme rabbi Aaron Shimon Spira, engraved on the edge of his tombstone dating from 1679. Though similar diversity of these relief signs and symbols can seldom be found at other cemeteries, the majority of rural Jewish cemeteries do display the general Jewish symbols of lions, crowns, grapes, money boxes, stars of David or pitchers and the blessing Kohens' hands in the most varied execution and shapes. Found far more frequently on tombstones in rural cemeteries are ornamental motifs taken from local forms of traditional folk art, such as floral ornaments, flower vases, garlands of fruit, eight-pointed stars, four-leafed clover, hearts and spiral shapes, which are absent from urban cemeteries. These simple tombstones thus become effective and interesting works of folk art.

During the period of upheaval around 1600 there appeared in Prague, too, an entirely new type of horizontal tombstone — a four-walled tomb with two high ends, somewhat reminiscent of the classical sarcophagus, known in Hebrew as an *ohel* — shrine or colloquially known as *hoysl* — little house, of which its construciton is reminiscent. These expensive tombstones were usually placed over the graves of very prominent spiritual and secular representatives of the community. Their construction provided more space for voluminous poetic texts praising the good deeds and the life of the deceased. The two oldest and largest tombstones are situated over the graves of two great figures of the Prague renaissance ghetto — Mordecai Maysl, primas of the Jewish Town, dating from 1601 and his contemporary Yehuda ben Bezalel, known as Rabbi Loew or also as MAHARAL mi Prag, of 1609. Some twenty other tombstones of this kind can be found at the Prague cemetery and they are also at the cemetery at Brandýs nad Labem, Heřmanův Městec, Golčův Jeníkov or, in Holešov, over the grave of rabbi Shabbatai ben Meir ha-Kohen known as SHAH, dating from 1662. Surprisingly, these tombstones were never popular in large centres of Jewish learning in Moravia — and are not to be found at Mikulov, Boskovice or Třebíč.

Throughout history, Prague has always been the largest Jewish community and the administrative centre for other Jewish communities in Bohemia. Understandably, there was a demand for a large number of good quality tombstones, and undoubtedly there was a stonecutter's workshop which continually made Jewish tombstones and perhaps nothing else. It was only this permanent production and specialization which was capable of maintaining the production of tombstones on such a high level, and of developing and expanding it. Tombstones of the so-called "Prague type" can be found in numerous cemeteries in Central Bohemia, usually over graves of the most prominent figures of local communities. It is easy to tell at first glance, from the material and execution, which tombstones were made to order in the Prague workshop to be delivered to the rural cemetery. More often, however, we notice the efforts of local stonecutters to imitate the Prague tombstones using a different material and a simplified form. Imported tombstones from Prague can be found at not so distant cemeteries in Dobříš, Mořina and Třebotov, as well as at more distant cemeteries of larger communities such as Kolín, Mladá Boleslav, Brandýs nad Labem, Březnice, Roudnice and elsewhere.

Around this Prague centre, the influence of which affected the entire central Bohemian region, it is possible to identify, from the kind of material used or the special decoration, certain peripheral groups which reveal a common tradition of stonecutting, or at least specific features of folk art in the given region. These groups are easier to define insofar as the tombstones demonstrate sufficiently marked specific features, while most of the simpler tombstones made locally in various periods are only similar in the use of material or in the dominant ornamental motifs.

A special, quite distinct group, is that of sandstone tombstones to be found at some cemeteries in Northeast Bohemia, markedly different in style, professional execution, rich composition, with a nearly sculpture like approach, wholly independent of the traditional type, with refined writing script and traditional Jewish symbols. According to execution and design these are evidently tombstones made to order at one of the local stonecutter's workshops known for its remarkable sculptures. The best examples can be found at Rychnov nad Kněžnou, at Dobruška and Vamberk. Similar tombstones of stylish and non-traditional form can now and then be found at other cemeteries in North Bohemia.

Another interesting and markedly distinct group are the asymmetric rococo tombstones of white marble found at numerous cemeteries in Eastern Bohemia. These tombstones manifest careful professional execution, the text is cut in fine lines into the stone and frequently decorated with minute floral ornaments, sometimes even

a family symbol, name or occupation. These tombstones are conspicuous because of the unusual shape and delicate execution. Their centre of production was most likely at Heřmanův Městec, and they can also be found at nearby graveyards at Golčův Jeníkov, Habry, Luže, Přestavlky, Hroubovice, Zájezdec, Hoješín, Dřevíkov and Zbraslavice.

Another interesting group can be identified in Southwest Bohemia, particularly from the use of the same material and prevailing style of decoration, revealing local traditions of folk art. These tombstones dating from the 18th and early 19th centuries are also made of white marble, but the inscription and ornaments are more rustic. A characteristic element of the decoration is the engraved ornament on the borders of the stelae, often decorated with floral motifs and stars. These tombstones are found mainly at the Jewish cemetery at Volyně, and further at Koloděje nad Lužnicí, Kasejovice, Rabí, Kolínec, Čichice, Osek near Strakonice, Čkyně near Vimperk and Vlachovo Březí.

The less distinct and more roughly executed the tombstones are, the more difficult it is to make comparisons, the similarity is confined to the same material and common decorative motifs. Such is the group of granite tombstones with marked rustic ornamentation, often of irregular shape, large plastic letters and shallow, often only engraved vegetable or geometric ornaments with hearts, eight-pointed stars and spirals, which we find throughout a strip of land stretching from Western Bohemia (the Tachov area, Drmoul, Chodová Planá, Blovice) to Southern Bohemia (Kamýk nad Vltavou, Březnice, Myslkovice, Ledeč nad Sázavou, Trhový Štěpánov, Lukavec).

The basic types of Jewish funereal plastic art and their evolution in Moravia is analogical to development in Bohemia. The medieval type of tombstone topped with a semi-circle or with bevelled corners is to be found here, as well as the block-like right-angled type of Renaissance tomb-stone with the inscription plaque in a semi-circle in the late variant dating from the early 17th century, which developed into the architectural type of a Baroque tombstone with semicolumns along both sides and finished with an elongated volute shield. It is evidently of some significance for the character of the ornamentation of tombstones as well as for that of other Jewish art in Moravia that there was none such centre of artistic development from which clearly defined artistic forms could be transferred to Jewish art as in Bohemia. On the contrary, development took place in a number of prospering Jewish communities in smaller towns, which favoured independence in their Jewish culture, quite often achieving original solutions.

In the 16th century, Mikulov became the administrative centre of Jewish communities in Moravia; even more distinct is this town's significance for the development of Jewish tombstones in the vast region of Southwest Moravia. The outstanding craftsmanship of the "Mikulov type" tombstones executed in white marble with neatly cut inscriptions can be found here, with examples of the block-like square Renaissance type dating from the 17th century to the architecturally composed tombstones with semicolumns and volute shields, topped with a central shell-shaped sculpture. Soon, however, this form was simplified, and ornamentation became limited to variations of the volute shield and to shell-shaped sculptures decorated with traditional Jewish motifs as well as with rich floral folk ornaments. Because of their distinct characteristics, the "Mikulov type" tombstones can easily be traced throughout the vast region of the Southwest part of Moravia (Třebíč, Velké Meziříčí, Lomnice, Boskovice, Dolní Kounice, Slavkov, Brno, Pohořelice, Bzenec, Brtnice, etc.) and reaching Bohemia as well (Jindřichův Hradec, Polná, Střítež). The exclusive incidence of this type at the cemetery of Mikulov unhesitatingly pinpoints this town as the site of the stonecutter's workshop, which for centuries uninterruptedly produced Jewish tombstones and supplied them to very distant communities. With all probability its field of activity included Austria and its products were evidently exported to Vienna.

A particular and quite unique example of a local type is the cemetery at Osoblaha, which with its marble tombstones is a site of specific differences in form, inscription and decoration. Tombstones of nearly square shape are topped with a semicircular shield with distinctive relief orna-

ments of traditional Jewish motifs (crown, lions, money-box, pitcher, blessing hands) and a comprehensive inscription in the lower part. Osoblaha, today situated on the Polish border, fell under the pronounced influence of Polish centres of traditional Jewish culture rather than Moravian ones, and the shape and decoration of tombstones are closely connected with it. At the cemetery in Osoblaha tombstones of this type are present exclusively and they are not found in any other Moravian cemetery.

The remaining part of Western and Central Moravia constitutes a large area with no incidence of similar clearly-defined characteristics. The tombstones in these cemeteries, mostly the work of local stonecutters, are usually of sandstone, of a simple shape with a semi-circular top, roughly worked, with large plastic inscriptions and often a rich floral decoration influenced by folk art. The most interesting cemeteries of this type are to the south of Ivančice, Úsov in Northern Moravia and Holešov in the east.

During the first half of the 19th century the Jewish tombstone continued in its traditional forms, particularly in rural areas with slower development. In aspects of form, however, greater uniformity inexorably set in as to form, in ornamentation and in the ever more advanced technical processing of stone, doing away with local peculiarities and specifics. This development of the traditional Jewish funereal art came to an end in the period of emancipation during the second half of the 19th century, when numerous new cemeteries were founded and a number of new communities were established; tombstones increasingly fell under the influence of non-Jewish funereal plastic art in form, material, ornamentation and ultimately in the very inscriptions, which by and by slide into German or Czech.

Equal rights of the Jews with the rest of the population in the Czech Lands were only recognized by the Austrian Constitution in 1848. This was followed by the abolition of forced residence

PÍSEČNÉ NAD DYJÍ

20

in ghettos and of the so-called familiant law, prohibiting free marriage, which immediately brought about marked demographic changes in the structure of the Jewish population in the Czech Lands. First of all Jewish families dispersed from the closed and cramped ghettos into the surrounding villages and towns, where many new Jewish communities were founded. In 1872 their number rose to some 330 communities and 50 religious societies. Simultaneously, the second half of the century marked a speedier growth of the Jewish population, which culminated in 1890, when there were 95,000 Jews in Bohemia and 45,000 in Moravia (a total of 140,000). At that time, however, Jewish families and individuals were in increasing numbers moving from previous rural communities to the towns and the newly budding trade and industrial centres. This migration brought about the gradual decline and extinction of numerous important historical rural settlements, where in the past only restrictive laws obliged the Jews to live, and gave rise to the founding of many new communities in large towns, from which until the middle of the 19th century Jews had been banned. On the basis of a law passed in 1890 on Jewish religious communities, in Bohemia there were only 197 and in Moravia 50 recognized Jewish religious communities (altogether 247). Migration to large towns resulted in the continuous fall in numbers of the Jewish population, accentuated in the 20th century by emigration overseas. By the end of the 1930s the number of Jews in Bohemia and Moravia had dropped to 118,000 as a result of emigration, low birth rates and fast assimilation. A total of 230 Jewish religious communities at that time took care of 430 cemeteries, of which nearly half ceased to serve their purpose and whose administration was taken over by others than the former Jewish community.

At the end of the Second World War, in view of the tremendous losses, it proved difficult to restore life in Jewish communities in the Czech Lands. For a short period 52 Jewish communities were restored only to become extinct as a result of emigration to Western Europe and, during the period 1948 to 1950, to Israel. During the war years the Nazis destroyed some 30 cemeteries, particularly in the Sudeten regions, and another 40 were intentionally devastated before the end of the war. Jewish rural settlement was practically not resumed after the war and care for cemeteries was taken over by old people, or else they were not cared for at all. In spite of the fact that under socialist rule cemeteries were for propaganda reasons formally protected, some further 45 cemeteries were abolished because of their state of disrepair during the postwar period, or were destroyed to give way to growing urban and communications development.

Today there are only five Jewish religious communities in Bohemia and Moravia—in Prague, Pilsen, Ústí nad Labem, Brno and Ostrava, and an additional four active religious societies in Karlovy Vary, Teplice, Liberec and Olomouc. But 334 Jewish cemeteries and some 20 Jewish departments in municipal cemeteries mostly founded in the 20th century still exist. Only 10 Jewish cemeteries are still used for burial, of the remaining only one-third is in a satisfactory state of repair, while the others are mostly deserted and left to ruin. Thus, they easily succumb to acts of vandalism. Tombstones and stones of the cemetery walls are stolen to serve as building material, usually ending with the total devastation of the cemetery by youngsters or local citizens. When no longer protected as monuments, they are ultimately abolished and liquidated with the approval of the Jewish community, as restoration would be too costly. The majority of Jewish cemeteries thus fade from memory. The ultimate testimony of a centuries' old history and of the life of onetime numerous rural Jewish communities in Bohemia and Moravia literally disappear before our eyes.

Arno Pařík

CHODOVÁ PLANÁ   26

DRMOUL

29 DLOUHÝ ÚJEZD

31   TELICE

NÝRSKO

CHLÍSTOV   38

HORAŽĎOVICE

DOLNÍ LUKAVICE

42

RADNICE

MERKLÍN

HŘEŠIHLAVY

RAKOVNÍK

48

KOŽLANY

HŘIVČICE   50

ČÍŽKOVICE

ROUDNICE NAD LABEM   52

BUDYNĚ NAD OHŘÍ

KOSTELEC U KŘÍŽKŮ   56

57

BRANDÝS NAD LABEM

PRAHA-ŽIŽKOV   60

PRAHA-SMÍCHOV

LITEŇ

MOŘINA

DOBŘÍŠ

ČELINA

NEVEKLOV

STUDENÝ

TRHOVÝ ŠTĚPÁNOV

BĚŠTÍN

69   DRAŽKOV

BOHOSTICE 72

KOSOVA HORA

MILEVSKO

VOTICE

76

PRUDICE

ČKYNĚ

STRÁŽ NAD NEŽÁRKOU   90

91   STARÉ MĚSTO POD LANDŠTEJNEM

OLŠANY
NOVÁ VČELNICE

DŘEVÍKOV

DŘEVÍKOV

DOBRUŠKA

116

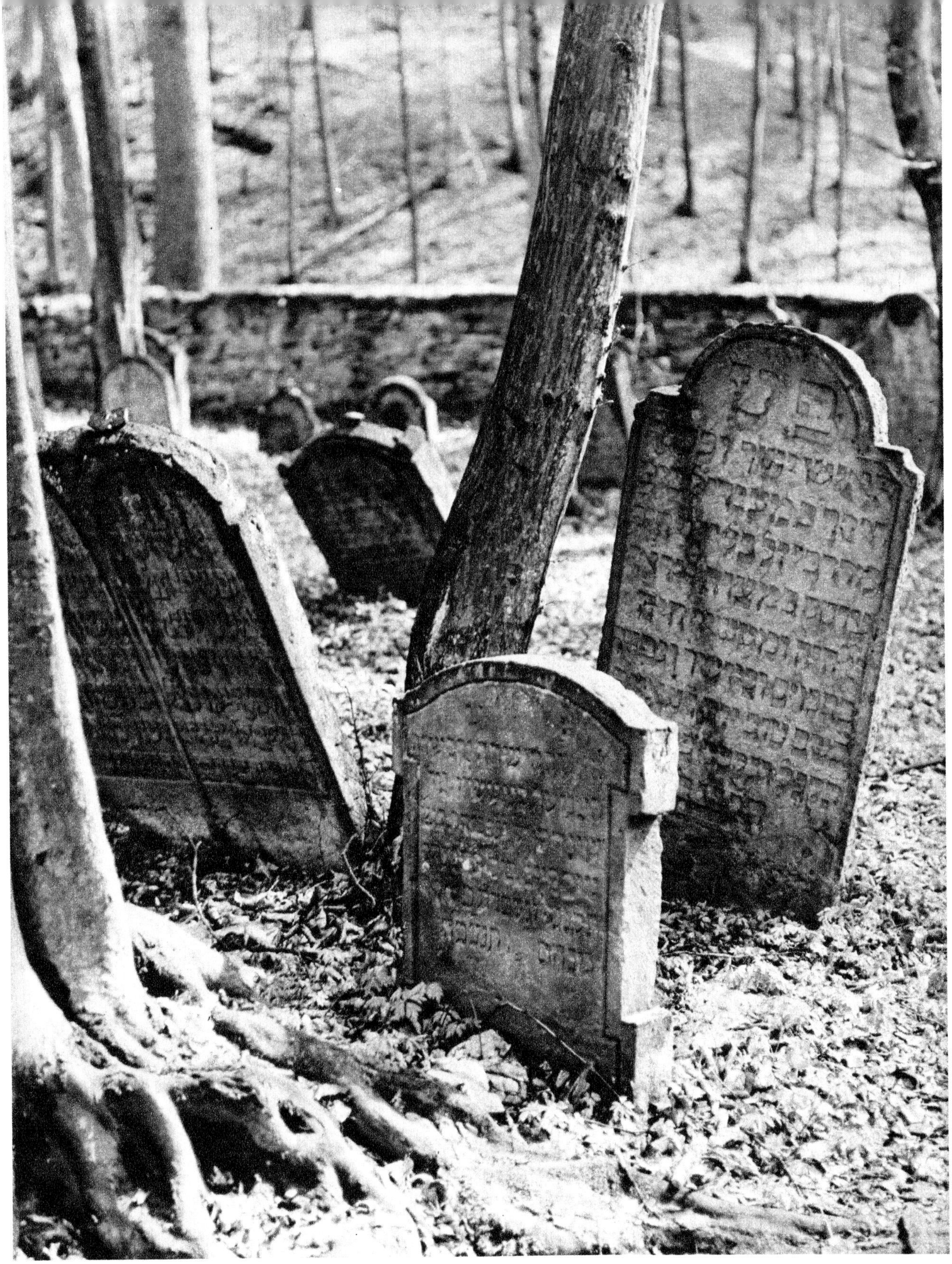

VELKÁ BUKOVINA
ROKYTNICE V ORLICKÝCH HORÁCH

VAMBERK   120

TŘEBÍČ

BATELOV

BRTNICE

LOMNICE U TIŠNOVA

SLAVKOV

ROUSÍNOV

138

BUČOVICE

UHERSKÝ BROD

LOŠTICE

HRANICE NA MORAVĚ

TOVAČOV

ÚSOV

OSOBLAHA

A LIST

of Jewish religious communities whose cemeteries are illustrated in the book. The author of the photographs has selected for this publication only photographs of cemeteries founded during the period of the ghettos before the Jewish population was granted equal civic rights, i. e. before the middle of the 19th century. An exception are the two younger cemeteries with tombstones transferred from abolished historical cemeteries (Mariánské Lázně and Uherský Brod) and the so-called New cemetery at Rožmberk nad Vltavou. The photographs were taken between 1984 and 1991, so that the present state of the cemeteries depicted may unfortunately no longer correspond with reality.

Geographical distances given in the list are measured as the crow flies.

ARNOLTOV (German name: Arnetzgrün, Arnitzgrün)
Village in W Bohemia, Sokolov district, 16 km NEE of
Cheb. Records of Jewish settlement before 1665, Jewish
community founded (f.) probably in 2nd half of 18th cent.,
abolished before 1878. — Cemetery W of village, at edge of
forest. F. probably in 18th cent., oldest preserved gravestones from early 19th cent. An abandoned small cemetery
with simple rustic-type gravestones. (p. 23)

BATELOV (G: Battelau)
Small town in W Moravia, 16 km SW of district capital Jihlava. Jewish settlement allegedly from 15th cent., Jewish
community of unknown age ceased to exist in World War II.
Small ghetto (valuable from the point of view of town-planning) with late 18th-cent. synagogue (now a gardeners'
club). — Important cemetery on hill W of town. Date of f.
unknown, oldest legible gravestone from 1715. In 1984,
cemetery provisionally fenced around. (p. 127)

BECHYNĚ (G: Bechin, Beching)
Town in S Bohemia, 20 km SW of district capital Tábor. Records of Jewish settlement from early 16th cent., Jewish
community f. probably in 1st half of 17th cent., ceased to
exist in World War II. Jewish street with mid-19th-cent.
synagogue (now museum of fire-fighting). — Cemetery NW
of town square, adjacent to town fortifications. F. in 1st half
of 17th cent., oldest legible gravestone from 1687. Well-
-maintained cemetery with valuable gravestones. (p. 79)

BĚŠTÍN (G: Biechtschin, Bieschtin)
Village in C Bohemia, 18 km SSW of district capital Beroun. Jewish settlement allegedly from 2nd half of 17th
cent., Jewish community of unknown age abolished after
1893. Small synagogue rebuilt as weekend house. — Cemetery NE of village, near the road to Hostomice. F. probably
in 1835, burials until World War II (mostly of people from
neighbouring Hostomice), from liberation in 1945 gradually
falling to ruins. (p. 68)

BLEVICE (G: Blewitz)
Village in C Bohemia, 12 km NE of district capital Kladno.
There was no Jewish community in Blevice where only one
Jewish family used to live for most of the time. — Cemetery
at S edge of village. F. allegedly in 17th cent., oldest legible
gravestone from 1720. From approx. 2nd half of 18th cent.
cemetery belonged to the community in the village of Ješín
(G: Jeschin, 7 km NW), in 20th cent. to the community of
Velvary (G: Welwarn, 8 km N). Grave-digger's house now
used as weekend cottage whose owners take care of the
cemetery. (p. 54)

BOHOSTICE (G: Bohostitz)
Village in C Bohemia, 14 km SE of district capital Příbram. Records of Jewish settlement from 1692, Jewish community f. probably in 18th cent., abolished probably in early 20th cent. Prayer room used to be in ordinary one-storey house. — Cemetery SW of village, at edge of forest. Date of f. unknown, oldest legible gravestone from 1748, last burial after 1930. A derelict village cemetery (p. 72)

BOSKOVICE (G: Boskowitz)
Town in NW Moravia, 13 km N of district capital Blansko. Jewish settlement from unknown date. Jewish community existed back in 15th cent., ceased to exist in World War II. Once among the largest and most important Jewish communities in Moravia. Large Jewish quarter of historical value with late-17th-cent. synagogue (now unused). — Cemetery at W edge of town. F. at unknown date, oldest preserved gravestones from late 17th cent., burials also after World War II. One of the largest and most valuable Jewish cemeteries in the Czech Lands. (p. 18, 131)

BRANDÝS NAD LABEM (G: Brandeis a. d. Elbe)
Town in C Bohemia, 20 km NE of centre of Prague. Jewish settlement probably from early 16th cent., records of existence of Jewish community from 1515, ceased to exist in World War II. Synagogue built in 1828—29 (now a storehouse). — Very valuable cemetery at NW edge of town. F. 1568, oldest legible gravestone from 1572, one tomb-sarcophagus. (p. 57)

BŘEZNICE (G: Bresnitz)
Town in SW Bohemia, 15 km SSW of district capital Příbram. Records of Jewish settlement from early 16th cent., Jewish community probably also from 16th cent., ceased to exist in World War II. Jewish quarter (ghetto) important from point of view of town-planning, with 18th-cent. synagogue, rebuilt after 1820 (now unused). — Very valuable cemetery 1.5 km N of town square. F. before 1617, oldest legible gravestones from late 17th cent. (p. 71)

BRTNICE (G: Pirnitz)
Small town in W Moravia, 12 km SE of district capital Jihlava. Jewish settlement from unknown date, Jewish community allegedly from 15th cent., ceased to exist in World War II. Small ghetto with 17th-cent. synagogue demolished in 1988. — Very valuable old cemetery 1 km NE of town square. F. before 1600, oldest legible gravestone from 1672, burials until 2nd half of 19th cent. Adjacent new cemetery f. in 2nd half of 19th cent. (p. 128)

BUČOVICE (G: Butschowitz)
Town in C Moravia, 14 km S of district capital Vyškov. Jewish settlement probably from 15th cent., Jewish community f. in 17th cent. at the latest, ceased to exist in World War II. Jewish quarter with synagogue built in 1853, demolished after 1965. — Cemetery in E part of town. F. at unknown date, oldest preserved gravestones from 18th cent. Cemetery resembles amphitheatre with gravestones placed on slopes surrounding a central area without gravestones. 19th-cent. ceremonial hall. (p. 139)

BUDYNĚ NAD OHŘÍ (G: Budin)

Town in N Bohemia, district of Litoměřice, 9 km SSW of Roudnice nad Labem. Records of Jewish settlement from 1st half of 16th cent., records of existence of Jewish community from early 17th cent., ceased to exist in World War II. Jewish street with 18th-cent. synagogue (now devastated and empty). — Cemetery 1 km SE of town, amidst fields. F. probably in 1785, oldest legible gravestone from 1798. Ceremonial hall and gate from 2nd half of 19th cent.

(p. 53)

BYŠICE (G: Bischitz)

Small town in C Bohemia, 10 km SE of district capital Mělník. Records of Jewish settlement from 1st quarter of 17th cent., existence of Jewish community not proved. — Cemetery N of local government office. F. allegedly in early 17th cent., oldest legible gravestone from 1723. A largely devastated cemetery with several valuable gravestones. (p. 55)

BZENEC (G: Bisenz)
Town in S Moravia, 17 km NE of district capital Hodonín. Jewish settlement from unknown date (allegedly from 14th cent.), existence of Jewish community documented from 2nd half of 16th cent., ceased to exist in World War II. Remains of Jewish quarter (synagogue built in 1863, demolished in 1960). — Cemetery E of town square, neighbours with communal cemetery. F. at unknown date, oldest preserved gravestones from late 17th cent., burials also after World War II. Ceremonial hall from 2nd half of 19th cent., repaired in 1985. (p. 141)

ČELINA (G: Tschelina)
Village in C Bohemia, district of Příbram, 12 km SE of Dobříš. Records of Jewish settlement from 1st quarter of 18th cent., Jewish community existing from unknown date abolished in late 19th cent. Small ghetto with synagogue adapted as private house. — Sloping cemetery SW of village. F. at unknown date, oldest legible gravestone from 1803, last burial in 1918. (p. 64, 157)

CHLÍSTOV (G: Chlistau, Klistau)
Village in SW Bohemia, 10 km SE of district capital Klatovy. Jewish settlement from unknown date, records of settlement and existence of Jewish community from 1st third of 19th cent. Jewish community abolished around 1900. Synagogue dating probably from 1st third of 19th cent. demolished after 1950. — Cemetery 1 km NE of village, on ridge of forested hill. F. at unknown date, oldest gravestones from approx. mid-19th cent. A derelict cemetery with very few gravestones. (p. 38)

CHODOVÁ PLANÁ (G: Kuttenplan)
Small town in W Bohemia, district of Tachov, 8 km SSE of Mariánské Lázně. Records of Jewish settlement from 2nd half of 16th cent., Jewish community f. allegedly in 1st half of 17th cent., existence documented from early 18th cent., abolished by the Nazis in 1938. Remains of Jewish street (synagogue from mid-18th cent., demolished after 1960). — Old cemetery at W edge of town, in chateau park. F. at unknown date, oldest preserved gravestones from 17th cent., burials probably until 1890. New cemetery f. 1890 (0.5 km S) destroyed by the Nazis. (p. 26)

ČICHTICE (G: Czichtitz, Tschichtitz)
Village in S Bohemia, district of Strakonice, 8 km SW of Vodňany. Records of Jewish settlement from 2nd half of 17th cent., existence of Jewish community documented from 1st quarter of 18th cent., abolished in late 19th cent. Two separate groups of former Jewish houses; prayer hall and school used to stand in Jewish street at W edge of village. —

Cemetery SE of village. F. probably in 2nd quarter of 18th cent., oldest legible gravestones from late 18th cent., burials until early 20th cent. Gravestones of south Bohemian type with plant motifs in ornaments. (p. 86)

ČÍŽKOVICE (G: Tschischkowitz)
Village in N Bohemia, district of Litoměřice, 4 km SW of Lovosice. Čížkovice had no Jewish community, it was inhabited by only a few Jewish families. — Small cemetery 1 km NW of village. F. 1800, oldest legible gravestone from 1839, burials probably until early 20th cent., mostly of people from the community in the village of Milešov (G: Mileschau, Milleschau, 9 km NW) and the garrison in Terezín (G: Theresienstadt, 9 km NE). Derelict, devastated cemetery. (p. 52)

ČKYNĚ (G: Tschkyn, Kieselhof)
Small town in S Bohemia, district of Prachatice, 8 km NE of Vimperk. Records of Jewish settlement from mid-16th cent., Jewish community from 1st half of 18th cent., its office transferred in 1897 to Vimperk (G: Winterberg). Synagogue built in 1828 (now empty, unused). — Cemetery SE of railway station. F. at unknown date, oldest legible gravestone from 1688, last burial in 1942. Well-maintained cemetery with gravestones of south Bohemian type. (p. 84)

DIVIŠOV
Small town in C Bohemia, 13 km E of district capital Benešov. Records of Jewish settlement from 2nd half of 17th cent., Jewish community f. 1776, abolished 1930. Mid-19th-cent. synagogue (now a hairdresser's). — Cemetery 2 km NE of village. F. probably 1776, oldest legible gravestones from late 18th cent. (p. 67)

DLOUHÁ VES (G: Altlangendorf)
Village in SW Bohemia, district of Klatovy, 4 km SSW of Sušice. Jewish settlement from unknown date, existence of Jewish community documented from 1st quarter of 18th cent., abolished probably in early 20th cent. Synagogue demolished after 1936. — Cemetery SE of village. F. at unknown date, documented in 1st quarter of 18th cent., oldest legible gravestone from 1742, burials until 1930s, then mostly of people from the community in Kašperské Hory (G: Bergreichenstein, 7 km SSE). Cemetery destroyed by the Nazis, its old part reconstructed in 1945. (p. 34)

DLOUHÝ ÚJEZD (G: Langendörflas)
Village in W Bohemia, 3 km S of district capital Tachov. Jewish settlement from unknown date, documented from early 17th cent., records of existence of Jewish community

153

from 1st quarter of 18th cent., abolished in late 19th cent. — Valuable cemetery W of village, at edge of forest. F. at unknown date, legible gravestones from 1st half of 18th cent., burials probably until late 19th cent. (p. 29)

DOBŘÍŠ (G: Dobrisch, Doberschisch)
Town in C Bohemia, 15 km NE of district capital Příbram. Jewish settlement from unknown date. Jewish community existed probably from 1st half of 17th cent., ceased to exist in World War II. Synagogue built in 1903—04 now adapted as community centre. — Cemetery 1.5 km NE of town square, on hill. F. at unknown date, oldest legible gravestone from 1650. Cemetery largely devastated at the time of Nazi occupation, area reduced after 1985. (p. 63)

DOBRUŠKA (G: Dobruschka, Gutenfeld)
Town in NE Bohemia, 16 km NW of district capital Rychnov nad Kněžnou. Records of Jewish settlement from 1st half of 16th cent., existence of Jewish community documented from 17th cent., ceased to exist in World War II. Synagogue from 2nd half of 19th cent. (now a church belonging to the Evangelical Church of Czech Brethren). — Cemetery at N edge of town, Křovická street. F. 1675, oldest preserved gravestones from late 17th cent. — Well-maintained cemetery with valuable gravestones. Relics related to former Jewish community displayed at former mortuary or hearse shed. (p. 116)

DOLNÍ BOLÍKOV (G: Wölking)
Village in SW Moravia, district of Jindřichův Hradec, 4 km NNE of Slavonice. Jewish settlement probably from 2nd half of 17th cent. Existence of Jewish community documented in early 18th cent., abolished in 1891. Synagogue demolished in 1900. — Cemetery W of village, at edge of forest. F. at unknown date, existence documented from 1st quarter of 18st cent., oldest gravestones from 18th cent., burials until early 20th cent. (p. 15, 93, 162)

DOLNÍ LUKAVICE (G: Unter-Lukawitz)
Village in SW Bohemia, district of Plzeň-South, 3 km NNE of Přeštice. Jewish settlement from early 17th cent., existence of Jewish community documented in 18th cent. (but probably older), abolished in late 19th cent. Synagogue rebuilt as private house. — Cemetery 1 km N of village, neighbours with communal cemetery. F. allegedly in 15th cent., oldest legible gravestone from 1711, burials until early 20th cent. (p. 42)

DOMOUSNICE (G: Domausnitz)
Village in NE Bohemia, 14 km SEE of district capital Mladá

Boleslav. Records of Jewish settlement from early 18th cent., existence of Jewish community documented in 1st half of 19th cent., abolished probably in late 19th cent. Prayer hall used to be in private house. — Cemetery in neighbouring village of Veselice (3 km NEE). F. at unknown date, oldest legible gravestone from 1831, burials until 1st third of 20th cent. Grave-digger's house now used as weekend cottage. (p. 113)

DRAŽKOV (G: Draschkow)
Village in S Bohemia, district of Příbram, 10 km W of Sedlčany. Jewish settlement from unknown date, existence of Jewish community documented in 1st half of 18th cent., abolished in late 19th cent. Mid-19th cent. synagogue rebuilt as local government office. — Valuable cemetery 2 km SW of village, in forest on Radobylka hill. F. at unknown date, oldest legible gravestone from 1681, last burial in 1936. The more recent burials also of people from the community of Kamýk nad Vltavou (G: Kameik, 2 km SW). Stone table used for ritual washing of the dead preserved in mortuary. (p. 69)

DŘEVÍKOV (G: Drewikau, Holzhof)
Village in E Bohemia, district of Chrudim, 5 km W of Hlinsko. Jewish settlement from unknown date, Jewish community f. probably in mid-18th cent., abolished around 1900. Jewish street with synagogue built in 2nd half of 18th cent., rebuilt as private house. — Cemetery NW of village, at edge of forest. F. probably in mid-18th cent., oldest preserved gravestone from 1762, burials until 1st third of 20th cent. Cemetery repaired in 1970s. Together with other Jewish relics in the village, cemetery is part of open-air ethnographic museum of Vysočina. (p. 108, 109)

DRMOUL (G: Dürrmaul)
Village in W Bohemia, district of Cheb, 4 km SW of Mariánské Lázně. Records of Jewish settlement from late 16th cent., Jewish community f. probably in 17th cent., abolished by the Nazis in 1938. Synagogue built in 1800—01, demolished in 1981. — Cemetery 1.5 km W of village on forested hill. F. at unknown date, oldest legible gravestones from late 17th cent. Very valuable cemetery with rustic-type gravestones whose design is very near to folk art. (p. 27, 149)

DUB
Village in S Bohemia, 10 km N of district capital Prachatice. Records of Jewish settlement from early 17th cent., Jewish community from early 18th cent., abolished in 1906. Jewish street with synagogue adapted as private house. — Cemetery 1 km S of village, on hill in forest. F. probably in 1706,

oldest legible gravestone from 1794, last burial in 1940.

(p. 86)

GOLČŮV JENÍKOV (G: Goltsch-Jenikau)

Town in E Bohemia, district of Havlíčkův Brod, 12 km SE of Čáslav. Jewish settlement probably from the Middle Ages, existence of Jewish community documented from mid-17th cent., abolished in World War II. Once an important Jewish community with famous yeshiva (rabbinic school). Jewish quarter with synagogue built in 1870—71 (now depository of the State Jewish Museum). — Cemetery at W edge of town. Allegedly of mediaeval origin, oldest legible gravestones from early 18th cent., last burial in 1941. Very valuable cemetery with three tombs-sarcophagi on graves of rabbis.

(p. 106)

HABRY (G: Habern)

Small town in E Bohemia, 18 km NW of district capital Havlíčkův Brod. Jewish settlement from unknown date, allegedly from the Middle Ages. Existence of Jewish community documented from 1st half of 17th cent., ceased to exist in World War II. Synagogue built in 1st half of 19th cent. (now a cinema). — Valuable cemetery 1 km NW of village. F. probably in 1st half of 17th cent., oldest legible gravestone from 1740.

(p. 105)

HEŘMANŮV MĚSTEC (G: Hermannstädtel)

Town in E Bohemia, 9 km W of district capital Chrudim. Jewish settlement documented from 1st half of 15th cent., Jewish community f. probably in 16th cent., ceased to exist in World War II. Remains of Jewish quarter, most of which was demolished after World War II, with synagogue built in 1870 (now a storehouse). — Cemetery at NE edge of town, Havlíčkova street. F. allegedly in 16th cent., oldest legible gravestone from 1647. Very valuable cemetery with several tombs-sarcophagi.

(p. 105)

HLUBOKÁ NAD VLTAVOU (formerly Podhradí, G: Podhrad, Frauenberg)

Town in S Bohemia, 9 km N of district capital České Budějovice. Jewish settlement from 1st half of 17th cent., existence of Jewish community documented from 2nd half of 17th cent., ceased to exist in World War II. Jewish street with synagogue built in 1907 (now chapel of the Czechoslovak Hussite Church). — Cemetery 0.5 km W of town, at Munický pond. F. in mid-18th cent., oldest legible gravestone from 1750.

(p. 88)

HOLEŠOV (G: Holleschau)

Town in C Moravia, 15 km NE of district capital Kroměříž.

Jewish settlement probably from 2nd half of 15th cent., existence of Jewish community documented from 1st half of 16th cent., ceased to exist in World War II. Once among the largest and most important Jewish communities in Moravia. Jewish quarter (ghetto) very interesting from architectural point of view, with synagogue built in 2nd half of 16th cent. (now houses the Moravian Jewish Museum). Second synagogue built in 1891—93, demolished by the Nazis. — Cemetery at N edge of Jewish town, Hankeho street. F. at unknown date, oldest legible gravestone from mid-17th cen-

tury, last burial in 1975. Very valuable cemetery with tomb-sarcophagus of famous rabbi Shah (born Sabbatai ben Meir ha-Kohen, d. 1662). (p. 143, 169)

HORAŽĎOVICE
Town in SW Bohemia, district of Klatovy, 16 km NW of Strakonice. Records of Jewish settlement from early 17th cent., existence of Jewish community documented from 1st half of 17th cent., ceased to exist in World War II. Synagogue built in 2nd half of 19th cent., demolished in 1980. — Cemetery 1 km N of town centre, f. in 1st third of 19th cent. In 1979, gravestones from an older abolished cemetery transferred here (oldest legible ones from 2nd half of 17th cent.) (p. 39)

HOŘICE (G: Horitz, Horschitz)
Town in NE Bohemia, 20 km SE of district capital Jičín. Records of Jewish settlement from early 17th cent., Jewish community f. probably in 2nd half of 17th cent., ceased to exist in World War II. Remains of Jewish quarter with 18th-cent. synagogue, rebuilt in 2nd half of 19th cent. (now chapel of the Czechoslovak Hussite Church). — Cemetery at N edge of town, Karlova street. F. allegedly in 2nd half of 17th cent., oldest preserved gravestones from late 18th cent., burials until 1897. Graves of Jewish soldiers killed in Napoleonic wars and the Prussia-Austria war of 1866. New cemetery of 1897 liquidated after 1965. (p. 115)

HORNÍ CEREKEV (G: Ober-Zerekwe, Lobeskirchen)
Small town in SE Bohemia, 14 km SE of district capital Pelhřimov. Records of Jewish settlement from mid-17th cent., Jewish community f. at unknown date (probably mid-18th cent.), ceased to exist in World War II. Synagogue built in 1867, demolished in 1951—52. — Cemetery 1.5 km NW of town square, at edge of forest. F. probably in 2nd half of 18th cent., oldest gravestones of baroque type. (p. 98)

HOŠTICE (G: Hostitz)
Village in S Bohemia, 7 km S of district capital Strakonice. Jewish settlement from unknown date, existence of Jewish community documented from 1st quarter of 18th cent., abolished in late 19th cent. Synagogue demolished around 1904. — Cemetery 1 km NW of village, at edge of forest. F. in 2nd quarter of 18th cent., oldest legible gravestone from 1735, burials probably until late 19th cent. (p. 85)

HRANICE (G: Mährisch-Weisskirchen)
Town in E Moravia, 23 km NE of district capital Přerov. Jewish settlement probably from 1611, existence of Jewish community documented from 1637, ceased to exist in World War II. Jewish street with synagogue built in 1863—64 (now bouses municipal museum). — Cemetery NE of town square, Palackého street. F. probably in mid-17th cent., oldest legible gravestone from 1686, last burial in 1956. In 1989, cemetery badly damaged; process of liquidation later halted and reconstruction now planned. (p. 145)

HŘEŠIHLAVY (G: Rescholau, Reschihlau, Herschichlau)
Village in C Bohemia, 20 km N of district capital Rokycany. Jewish settlement probably from 1st half of 17th cent., Jewish community allegedly existed from late 17th cent., documented from 2nd half of 18th cent., abolished in late 19th cent. Jewish street (synagogue demolished probably in early 20th cent.). — Cemetery 0.5 km E of village, on forested slope. F. in 1821, oldest legible gravestone from 1826, burials until 1930s. (p. 46)

HŘIVČICE (G: Riwtschitz, Pflanzendorf)
Village in C Bohemia, 8 km SE of district capital Louny. Jewish community probably never existed in Hřivčice, and only one or two Jewish families lived there. — Valuable cemetery 1 km S of village, on hill near railway line. F. probably in mid-18th cent., oldest legible gravestone from 1759, burials until around 1st third of 20th cent. Cemetery belonged to Jewish community in the village of Hříškov (G: Rischkau, 6 km SW) and was also used by communities in Panenský Týnec (G: Jungfernteinitz, Jungferteinitz, 4 km S) and Ročov (G: Unter-Rotschow, Unter-Rotschau, 13 km SW) (p. 50)

HUMPOLEC (G: Gumpolds)
Town in SE Bohemia, 15 km NE of district capital Pelhřimov. Records of Jewish settlement from 2nd half of 14th cent. (later disappeared), new Jewish settlement from 1st quarter of 17th cent., existence of Jewish community documented from 1st quarter of 18th-cent., ceased to exist in World War II. Jewish quarter (ghetto) with 18th cent. synagogue, rebuilt in 2nd half of 19th cent. (now chapel of the Czechoslovak Hussite Church). — Valuable cemetery 1 km NE of town centre. F. in 1st quarter of 18th cent., oldest legible gravestones from mid-18th cent. (p. 100)

IVANČICE (G: Eibenschitz, Eibenschütz)
Town in SW Moravia, 20 km SW of district capital Brno. Jewish settlement from unknown date (allegedly existed in 13th cent.), documented from 2nd half of 15th cent. Existence of Jewish community documented from 2nd half of 16th cent., ceased to exist in World War II. Jewish street with synagogue built in 1853 (now a storehouse). — Cemetery 0.5 km NW of town centre, Mřenková street. F. prob-

ably in 16th cent., oldest legible gravestone from 1552, burials also after World War II. Very valuable, well-maintained cemetery. (p. 136)

JIČÍN (G: Gitschin)
District capital in NE Bohemia. Records of Jewish settlement from 2nd half of 14th cent., Jewish community probably from 17th cent., ceased to exist in World War II. Jewish street with synagogue built probably in 18th cent. (now a storehouse). — Valuable cemetery 2 km NE of town square, amidst fields. F. in 1651, oldest gravestone from 17th cent., last burial in 1949. (p. 115)

JINDŘICHŮV HRADEC (G: Neuhaus)
District capital in S Bohemia. Jewish settlement probably from late 13th cent., existence of Jewish community documented from late 16th cent., ceased to exist in World War II. Jewish street with 18th-cent. synagogue, rebuilt in 1867 (now chapel of the Czechoslovak Hussite Church). — Valuable cemetery 1.5 km SSW of town centre, on hill overlooking Nežárka river. F. allegedly in 1400, oldest legible gravestone from 1714, burials also after World War II. Modern ceremonial hall of 1937 with original furnishings. (p. 93)

JISTEBNICE (G: Gistebnitz, Jistebnitz)
Small town in S Bohemia, 12 km NW of district capital Tábor. Records of Jewish settlement from 1st half of 16th cent., existence of Jewish community documented from 1st half of 17th cent., abolished after 1930. — Very valuable cemetery 1.5 km WSW of town square, amidst fields. F. at unknown date, oldest legible gravestone from 1640, burials until World War II. Stone table for ritual washing of the dead preserved in mortuary. (p. 78, 158)

KAMENICE NAD LIPOU (G: Kamenitz a. d. Linde)
Town in S Bohemia, 18 km NW of district capital Pelhřimov. Records of Jewish settlement from mid-17th cent., existence of Jewish community documented from 2nd half of 17th cent., ceased to exist in World War II. Synagogue built in 1937—38, the most recent synagogue on the territory of Czechoslovakia (now chapel of the Evangelical Church of Czech Brethren). — Cemetery 1.5 km NE of town square, at edge of forest. F. in early 19th cent., oldest legible gravestone from 1807. (p. 96)

KAMENNÁ
Village in C Bohemia, 7 km SSW of district capital Příbram. Records of Jewish settlement from 2nd half of 17th cent., Jewish community f. probably in 1709, abolished probably in late 19th cent. Prayer hall adapted as garage. — Cemetery 0.5 km NNW of village, at edge of forest. F. probably after mid-18th cent., oldest legible gravestone from 1762, burials until 1930s. (p. 71)

KASEJOVICE
Small town in SW Bohemia, district of Plzeň-South, 16 km N of Horažďovice. Records of Jewish settlement from 2nd half of 16th cent., existence of Jewish community documented from 1st quarter of 17th cent., abolished after 1921. Re-

ČELINA

mains of ghetto (important from point of view of town-planning) with 18th-cent. synagogue (now houses municipal museum). — Valuable cemetery 0.5 km NNW of town square, on hill. F. probably in 1704, oldest legible gravestone from 1710, burials until World War II. (p. 40)

KOLÍN

District capital in C Bohemia. Records of Jewish settlement from early 14th cent., existence documented from 1st half of 15th cent., abolished after 1950. Once ranked among most important Jewish communities in Bohemia. Jewish street with 17th-cent., synagogue (now empty, unused). — Very

valuable old cemetery WNW of town square, between Kmochova and Sluneční streets. F. allegedly in 1418, oldest legible gravestones from 1492, burials until 1887. New cemetery f. in 1887, burials also after World War II. (p. 110)

KOLINEC

Small town in SW Bohemia, 15 km SE of district capital Klatovy. Records of Jewish settlement from mid-17th cent. (probably much older). Existence of Jewish community documented from 1st quarter of 18th cent., abolished in early 20th cent. Early 19th-cent. synagogue demolished after 1930. — Valuable cemetery at SE edge of town, on steep

slope. F. allegedly in 14th cent., oldest legible gravestone from 1727, burials until World War II. (p. 34)

KOLODĚJE NAD LUŽNICÍ (G: Kaladei, Kalladay)
Village in S Bohemia, district of České Budějovice, 3 km N of Týn nad Vltavou. Records of Jewish settlement from 1st half of 17th cent., Jewish community f. in late 17th cent., ceased to exist in World War II. In 19th cent., Jews represented half of the village's population. Late 17th-cent. synagogue demolished in 1948. — Valuable cemetery at N edge of village. F. around 1700, oldest legible gravestone from 1734. South Bohemian type gravestones with plant motifs in ornaments. (p. 81)

KORYČANY (G: Koritschan)
Town in S Moravia, district of Kroměříž, 11 km NNE of Kyjov. Records of Jewish settlement from 2nd half of 16th cent., Jewish community f. probably in 1st half of 17th cent., abolished around 1900. Jewish street with synagogue rebuilt as shop. — Cemetery at E edge of town. F. at unknown date, oldest legible gravestone from 1630, burials until World War II. Devastated cemetery with valuable gravestones. (p. 141)

KOŠETICE
Village in SE Bohemia, 16 km NW of district capital Pelhřimov. Records of Jewish settlement from 1st half of 17th cent., existence of Jewish community documented only from 1st half of 19th cent. (probably much older), abolished probably around 1900. Synagogue rebuilt as private house. — Cemetery 1 km SE of town, in forest. F. at unknown date, oldest gravestones from late 17th cent. (p. 102)

KOSOVA HORA (G: Amschelberg)
Small town in C Bohemia, district of Příbram, 3 km E of Sedlčany. Records of Jewish settlement from 2nd half of 16th cent., existence of Jewish community documented from 2nd half of 17th cent., abolished in late 19th cent. Jewish quarter (ghetto) important from point of view of town-planning, with synagogue built probably in 18th cent. (now empty, unused). — Cemetery S of town. F. allegedly in 1580, oldest legible gravestone from 1780, burials until World War II. (p. 73)

KOSTELEC U KŘÍŽKŮ (G: Kreuz-Kosteletz)
Village in C Bohemia, district of Prague-East, 12 km SW of Říčany. Jewish settlement from unknown date, documented together with existence of Jewish community from 1st quarter of 18th cent. Jewish community abolished in late 19th cent. Small synagogue demolished after World War II. — Cemetery 1 km WSW of village. F. at unknown date, oldest

legible gravestone from 1724, burials (of people living in region between S outskirts of Prague and Sázava river) until World War II. (p. 56)

KOŽLANY (G: Koslan, Koschlan)
Town in W Bohemia, district of Plzeň-North, 4 km NE of Kralovice. Existence of Jewish settlement and Jewish community documented from 2nd half of 17th cent., community probably ceased to exist in 1st half of 18th cent. — Cemetery 1.5 km NW of town, on hill, surrounded by quarry. F. at unknown date, oldest legible gravestone from 1717, burials until World War II. Cemetery belonged to Jewish community in the village of Kůzová (G: Wallisgrün, Wallisdorf, 5 km NNW) from 2nd half of 18th cent. (p. 49)

KRÁSNÁ LÍPA (G: Schönlind)
No longer existing village in W Bohemia, district of Sokolov, 18 km ENE of Cheb, 2 km SE of Kostelní Bříza. Records of Jewish settlement from 16th cent., existence of Jewish community documented from 1st half of 18th cent., abolished in late 19th cent. Remains of Jewish quarter flooded by dammed brook after 1962. — Cemetery on slope overlooking dam. F. at unknown date, oldest legible gravestone from 1784, burials probably until late 19th cent. (p. 23)

KYNŠPERK NAD OHŘÍ (G: Königsberg a.d. Eger)
Town in W Bohemia, district of Sokolov, 12 km NE of Cheb. Jewish settlement from unknown date, documented from mid-14th cent., Jewish community probably from 14th cent., abolished in 1930. Early 19th-cent. synagogue destroyed by the Nazis in 1938. — Cemetery at N edge of inner town, on slope of castle hill. F. allegedly in mid-14th cent., oldest legible gravestone from 1st half of 17th cent., last burial in 1949. (p. 3)

LEDEČ NAD SÁZAVOU
Town in SE Bohemia, 24 km NW of district capital Havlíčkův Brod. Records of Jewish settlement from 1st quarter of 16th cent., existence of Jewish community documented from early 17th cent., ceased to exist in World War II. Synagogue built probably in 18th cent. (now unused). — Cemetery 0.5 km SW of town square, neighbours with communal cemetery. F. in early 17th cent., oldest preserved gravestones from 2nd half of 17th cent. Very valuable but largely devastated cemetery. (p. 102)

LIBOCHOVICE
Town in N Bohemia, 15 km SSW of district capital Litoměřice. Records of Jewish settlement from 2nd half of 15th cent., Jewish community f. probably in 2nd half of 16th

cent., ceased to exist in World War II. Jewish quarter (18th-
-cent. synagogue demolished in 1985). — Very valuable
cemetery about 1 km NW of town square, near communal
cemetery. F. in 1583, oldest legible gravestone from 1588.

(p. 51)

LITEŇ (G: Litten)
Small town in C Bohemia, 8 km SE of district capital Beroun. Jewish settlement from unknown date, documented

from 17th cent. Existence of Jewish community documented
from 1st quarter of 18th cent., abolished after 1930. 19th-
-cent. synagogue rebuilt as headquarters of firemen's corps.
— Valuable cemetery 1 km S of town square. F. in 1680, oldest gravestones from late 17th cent., burials until World
War II.

(p. 62)

LOMNICE U TIŠNOVA
Small town in W Moravia, district of Blansko, 6 km N of
Tišnov. Jewish settlement from unknown date, documented
from mid-17th cent. Jewish community f. in 1st quarter of
18th cent., abolished in 1919. Jewish quarter (ghetto) important from point of view of town-planning, with 18th-
-cent. synagogue (now a storehouse). — Valuable cemetery
0.5 km N of town square. F. in 1st quarter of 18th cent., oldest legible gravestone from 1716, burials until World
War I.

(p. 129)

LOŠTICE (G: Loschitz)
Town in N Moravia, district of Šumperk, 12 km NW of Li-
tovel. Records of Jewish settlement from 1st half of 16th
cent., existence of Jewish community documented from 2nd
half of 16th cent., ceased to exist in World War II. Jewish
quarter with early 19th-cent. synagogue (now a music
school). — Valuable cemetery about 1 km SE of town
square. F. in 1554, oldest preserved gravestones from 17th
cent., a tomb-sarcophagus from 1st half of 18th cent.

(p. 145)

LOUČIM (G: Lautschim)
Village in SW Bohemia, 16 km SE of district capital Domaž-
lice. Jewish settlement from unknown date, documented
from 1st quarter of 18th cent. Jewish community f. probably
in 1st half of 19th cent., abolished in 1894. Prayer room
used to be in private house. — Cemetery about 1.5 km NE
of village, in forest. F. probably in 1842, last burial in 1948.
Burials mostly of people from the communities of Kdyně (G:
Neugedein, 6 km NW) and Všeruby (G: Neumark, 9 km
SW).

(p. 32)

LUKAVEC
Small town in SE Bohemia, district of Pelhřimov, 17 km SE
of Vlašim. Jewish settlement existed probably in 1st half of
16th cent., documented together with existence of Jewish
community from 1st quarter of 18th cent. Jewish community
abolished probably around 1900. Synagogue built probably
in early 19th cent., demolished in 1952. — Cemetery 150 m
N of town square, amidst gardens. F. at unknown date, existence documented in 1st quarter of 18th cent., oldest legible
gravestone from 1725, last burial in 1935.

(p. 102)

LUŽE

Small town in E Bohemia, 18 km ESE of district capital Chrudim. Records of Jewish settlement from late 16th cent., Jewish community f. probably in 17th cent., ceased to exist in World War II. Jewish street with 18th-cent. synagogue (now skin drying house). — Valuable cemetery about 1.5 km NEE of town square, at edge of forest. F. at unknown date, oldest preserved gravestones from 17th cent. (p. 111)

MARIÁNSKÉ LÁZNĚ (G: Marienbad)

Town in W Bohemia, 25 km SE of district capital Cheb. Jewish settlement and Jewish community from 1st quarter of 19th cent., community abolished by the Nazis in 1938. Synagogue built in 1883—84, destroyed by the Nazis in 1938. — Cemetery 2 km SW of centre, on slope rising from Chebská street, near railway line. F. probably in 1875, still used for burials. Cemetery almost totally destroyed by the Nazis. Several dozen valuable gravestones transferred after 1987 from Tachov. Two valuable gravestones (see photo) one of them dating from 1714, transferred after 1976 from the town of LÁZNĚ KYNŽVART (G: Königswart, 6 km NW). Existence of Jewish community in Lázně Kynžvart documented from early 15th cent., abolished after 1921. Small remains of ghetto. 18th-cent. synagogue destroyed in 1938 by the Nazis. — Cemetery of mediaeval origin, with gravestones from 16th cent., destroyed by the Nazis. (p. 24)

MARKVAREC (G: Markwarding, Markwaretz)

Village in SW Moravia, district of Jindřichův Hradec, 14 km SW of Telč. Jewish settlement from unknown date, documented from 2nd half of 18th cent. Jewish community f. probably in 2nd half of 18th cent., abolished in 1888. Jewish quarter with ruins of late 18th-cent. synagogue. — Cemetery 700 m SE of village green, in forest. F. in 1794, oldest legible gravestone from 1802. (p. 94)

MERKLÍN

Small town in SW Bohemia, district of Plzeň-South, 10 km SWW of Přeštice. Jewish settlement from unknown date. Jewish community f. probably in 18th cent., abolished in early 20th cent. Synagogue built in 1st half of 19th cent. rebuilt as private house. — Cemetery 2.5 km S of town square, in forest. F. at unknown date, oldest preserved gravestones probably from late 18th cent., burials until World War II. (p. 46)

MIKULOV (G: Nikolsburg)

Town in S Moravia, 18 km WNW of district capital Břeclav. Records of Jewish settlement from 1st half of 15th cent., Jewish community f. probably in 15th cent., existence docu-mented from 1st half of 16th cent., abolished by the Nazis in 1938. Once the most important Jewish community in Moravia, from 16—19th cent. the residence of provincial rabbis. Second (after Prague) most numerous Jewish community in the Czech Lands. Remains of large, architecturally important Jewish town (ghetto) with synagogue built probably in 16th cent., rebuilt in 1st half of 18th cent. (now a concert hall). Other synagogues demolished after World War II. — Large cemetery 300 m N of town square. F. at unknown date, oldest legible gravestone from 1605, burials also after World War II. Very valuable cemetery with some 2,500 gravestones. Their ornaments and artistic design served as example for other cemeteries in S Moravia. Ceremonial hall of 1895. (p. 135)

MILEVSKO (G: Mühlhausen)

Town in S Bohemia, 22 km NE of district capital Písek. Records of Jewish settlement from mid-17th cent., Jewish community f. probably in 2nd half of 17th cent., ceased to exist in World War II. Old synagogue built probably in 18th cent. (now cellar of private house), new synagogue built in 1914—19 (now chapel of the Czechoslovak Hussite Church). — Valuable cemetery 2 km NEE of town square, at edge of forest. F. in 1714 (oldest gravestone from that year), burials until World War II. (p. 76)

MIROTICE

Town in S Bohemia, 15 km NNW of district capital Písek. Records of Jewish settlement from 1st half of 16th cent., existence of Jewish community documented from 2nd half of 17th cent., abolished in late 19th cent. 18th-cent. synagogue destroyed in 1945 air raid. — Cemetery 300 m N of town square, on slope rising from Neradovská street. F. allegedly in 1681 (but oldest gravestone dated 1647), last burial in 1946. Valuable, well-preserved cemetery. (p. 74)

MIROVICE

Town in S Bohemia, 22 km NNW of district capital Písek. Records of Jewish settlement from 2nd half of 16th cent., Jewish community f. probably in late 17th cent., abolished after 1921. Synagogue rebuilt as private house. — Cemetery about 1 km N of town, on slope overlooking Skalice river. F. at unknown date, existence documented in 1st quarter of 18th cent., oldest legible gravestone from 1764, burials until World War II. (p. 74)

MLADÁ BOLESLAV (G: Jungbunzlau)

District capital in C Bohemia. Records of Jewish settlement from 2nd half of 15th cent., existence of Jewish community documented from 2nd half of 16th cent., ceased to exist in

World War II. Once an important centre of Jewish culture and Hebrew letterpress printing. Remains of Jewish quarter (18th-cent. synagogue demolished in 1958). — Very valuable cemetery 300 m SW of town square, on slope. F. at unknown date, existence documented in 1584, oldest legible gravestone from 1604, burials also after World War II. Renaissance gravestone of financier Jacob Bassevi von Treuenberg, first Jew raised to nobility in the Habsburg empire (d. 1634). Octagonal ceremonial hall. (p. 113)

MLADÁ VOŽICE (G: Jung-Woschitz)
Town in SE Bohemia, 16 km NE of district capital Tábor. Records of Jewish settlement from mid-17th cent., existence of Jewish community documented from early 18th cent., ceased to exist in World War II. 19th-cent. synagogue demolished after 1960. — Cemetery 4 km NE of town, between Elbančice estate and the village of Vilice, at edge of forest. F. at unknown date, existence documented in 1st quarter of 18th cent., oldest preserved gravestones from 18th cent. (p. 79)

MOŘINA (G: Gross-Morschin, Gross-Morzin)
Village in C Bohemia, 10 km E of district capital Beroun. Records of Jewish settlement from 1st quarter of 18th cent., Jewish community f. probably in 2nd half of 18th cent., abolished in 1908. Synagogue built probably in 19th cent., rebuilt as private house. — Cemetery 1 km NW of church, on hillside. F. in 1735—36, oldest legible gravestone from 1741, burials until 1930s. Mortuary with Latin-Hebrew memorial plaque from the time of the foundation of the cemetery. (p. 62)

MYSLKOVICE (G: Miskowitz)
Village in S Bohemia, 14 km SE of district capital Tábor. Records of Jewish settlement from 1st half of 17th cent., Jewish community f. in 2nd half of 18th cent., abolished af-

ter 1921. Large Jewish quarter (most of the village's population in the 19th cent. were Jews). Ruins of 18th-cent. synagogue demolished in 1965. — Cemetery 0,5 km NE of village, at edge of forest. F. allegedly in 1770, oldest preserved gravestones probably from late 18th cent., burials until World War II. Renovated, well-maintained cemetery.

(p. 83)

NEVEKLOV
Town in C Bohemia, 12 km SW of district capital Benešov. Jewish settlement from unknown date, documented from early 17th cent. Jewish community f. probably in 1st half of 17th cent., ceased to exist in World War II. 17th-cent. synagogue rebuilt in 18th cent. (now a storehouse). — Cemetery 800 m SSE of town square. F. probably in 1755, oldest legible gravestone from time of foundation. (p. 65)

NEZNAŠOV
Village in S Bohemia, district of České Budějovice, 3 km W of Týn nad Vltavou. Jewish settlement probably from 1678, Jewish community f. probably in late 17th cent., abolished after 1890. Once a majority Jewish population, original houses still preserved. Ruins of early 18th-cent. synagogue demolished in 1973. — Cemetery 600 m SE of village. F. in 2nd quarter of 18th cent., oldest legible gravestone from 1749, burials until 1930s. (p. 81)

NOVÁ CEREKEV (G: Neu-Zerekwe)
Small town in SE Bohemia, 8 km W of district capital Pelhřimov. Jewish settlement from unknown date, probably from 2nd half of 17th cent. Jewish community f. allegedly in late 17th cent., abolished in late 19th cent. Small Jewish quarter with mid-19th-cent. synagogue (now a storehouse). — Cemetery at NE edge of village. F. in late 17th cent., oldest legible gravestone from 1692. Burials until World War II, mostly of people from the community of Pelhřimov (G: Pilgrams). (p. 100)

NOVÁ VČELNICE (formerly Nový Etynk, G: Neu-Ötting)
Small town in SE Bohemia, 11 km NE of district capital Jindřichův Hradec. Jewish settlement from unknown date, documented from 1st quarter of 18th cent. Existence of Jewish community documented from 2nd quarter of 18th cent., abolished in 1893. Early 19th-cent. synagogue rebuilt as residential house. — Cemetery 800 m E of town square, adjacent to road. F. in 1800, oldest legible gravestone from 1830, burials until 1930s. (p. 94)

NOVÉ SEDLIŠTĚ (G: Neu-Zedlisch)
Village in W Bohemia, 8 km SE of district capital Tachov.

Records of Jewish settlement from early 17th cent., existence of Jewish community documented from 1st quarter of 18th cent., abolished in 1914. 18th-cent. synagogue demolished after World War I. — Valuable cemetery 0.5 km WNW of chateau. F. at unknown date, oldest legible gravestone from 1704, burials until 1930s. (p. 30)

NÝRSKO (G: Neuern)
Town in SW Bohemia, 16 km SW of district capital Klatovy. Records of Jewish settlement from early 17th cent. (allegedly much older), existence of Jewish community documented from 1st quarter of 18th cent., abolished by the Nazis in 1938. Small remains of ghetto (late 18th-cent. synagogue demolished after 1956). — Cemetery 1 km SE of town square, near road to the village of Milence, amidst fields. F. at unknown date, oldest legible gravestone from 1715. (p. 33)

OLŠANY (G: Wolschan)
Village in SW Moravia, 18 km E of district capital Jindřichův Hradec. Jewish settlement from unknown date, documented from 2nd half of 18th cent. Jewish community f. probably in 18th cent., abolished in late 19th cent. Wooden synagogue destroyed by fire in 1928. — Cemetery 0.5 km SE of village, on hill in small forest. F. in 18th cent., burials until 1st third of 20th cent. (p. 94)

OSOBLAHA (G: Hotzenplotz)
Small town in NE Silesia, district of Bruntál, 20 km N of Krnov. Jewish settlement from 1st half of 14th cent., Jewish community f. probably in 15th cent., abolished in early 20th cent. Once a large Jewish community. Early 19th-cent. synagogue demolished in 1933. — Cemetery NE of town square, adjacent to the outer side of town fortifications. F. probably in 15th cent., oldest preserved gravestones from 2nd half of 17th cent., burials probably until 1930s. Cemetery badly damaged by 1945 war events but still a very valuable relic with Polish-type gravestones that are unique on Czechoslovak territory. (p. 147)

PAVLOV
Village in SE Bohemia, 4 km SSE of district capital Pelhřimov. Records of Jewish settlement from 1st half of 17th cent., existence of Jewish community from 1st half of 19th cent., abolished probably in late 19th cent. Prayer room used to be in private house. — Small cemetery 0.5 km SE of village, adjacent to road. F. at unknown date, oldest legible gravestone from 1804, burials allegedly until World War I. (p. 98)

PÍSEČNÉ (G: Piesling)

Small town in SW Moravia, district of Jindřichův Hradec, 9 km SE of Slavonice. Records of Jewish settlement from 1700, existence of Jewish community documented from 1727, abolished by the Nazis in 1938. Jewish quarter (18th--cent. synagogue demolished in 1948). — Valuable cemetery 0.5 km SW of town. F. probably in 1st half of 18th cent., oldest legible gravestone from 1733. (p. 20, 93)

PODBŘEZÍ

Village in NE Bohemia, 12 km NW of district capital Rychnov nad Kněžnou. Jewish settlement allegedly from 1696. Existence of Jewish community documented from 1st quarter of 18th cent., abolished in 1893. Small 19th-cent. synagogue adapted as private house. — Valuable cemetery 0.5 km NE of village, 0.5 km E of Skalka chateau, in forest near stream. F. at unknown date, oldest legible gravestone from 1725, last burial in 1924. (p. 117)

PODIVÍN (G: Kostel)

Town in S Moravia, 8 km NNW of district capital Břeclav. Jewish settlement from unknown date, Jewish community existed allegedly in early 17th cent., documented from 2nd half of 17th cent., ceased to exist in World War II. Two separate Jewish quarters (synagogue built probably in 17th cent., demolished after 1945). — Cemetery 0.5 km N of town square. F. probably in 2nd half of 17th cent., oldest legible gravestone from late 17th cent., burials also after World War II. (p. 136)

PODMOKLY

Village in SW Bohemia, district of Klatovy, 4 km E of Sušice. Records of Jewish settlement from last quarter of 17th cent., existence of Jewish community documented from 1st quarter of 18th cent., abolished probably in late 19th cent. Jewish quarter with synagogue adapted as private house. — Cemetery 1 km NW of village green, on hillside at edge of forest. F. at unknown date, existence documented in 1st quarter of 18th cent., oldest legible gravestone from 1732, burials probably until early 20th cent. (p. 36)

POHOŘELICE (G: Pohrlitz)

Town in S Moravia, district of Břeclav, 25 km SSW of centre of Brno. Records of Jewish settlement from late 15th cent. Jewish community probably existed then, documented again from 1st half of 17th cent., abolished by the Nazis in 1938. Remains of Jewish quarter (mid-19th-cent. synagogue demolished by the Nazis). — Valuable cemetery 400 m NW of town square, Tyršova street. F. at unknown date, oldest preserved gravestone from 2nd half of 17th cent.

(p. 16, 135)

POLICE (G: Pullitz)

Village in SW Moravia, district of Třebíč, 7 km SE of Jemnice. Jewish settlement allegedly from 15th cent., documented from 2nd half of 17th cent. Jewish community allegedly existed in 1st half of 16th cent., documented from early 18th cent., abolished in late 19th cent. Jewish street with synagogue of 1759, adapted as a Sokol gymnasium. — Valuable cemetery at S edge of village. Existed allegedly in 1st half of 16th cent., oldest legible gravestone from 1681, burials until early 20th cent. (p. 125)

POLNÁ

Town in SE Bohemia, 14 km NE of district capital Jihlava. Records of Jewish settlement from 1st half of 16th cent., existence of Jewish community documented from late 16th cent., ceased to exist in World War II. Jewish town (ghetto) important from point of view of town-planning, with ruins of 17th-cent. synagogue (roof collapsed in 1969). — Valuable cemetery 700 m NW of town square. Existence documented in late 16th cent., oldest legible gravestone from 1683. (p. 123)

PRAGUE (G: Prag, in Czech: Praha)

Town in C Bohemia, capital of Czechoslovakia and the Czech Republic. Jewish settlement from unknown date, Jewish community existed probably as early as 11th cent., existence documented from 12th cent., active to date. From the Middle Ages, one of the most numerous and most important Jewish communities in Europe, centre of Jewish culture, arts and crafts, etc. Headquarters of the Federation of Jewish Communities in the Czech Republic. — Of the old large ghetto with 9 synagogues (known as Jewish Town-Židovské Město or Josefov) demolished in early 20th cent., 6 synagogues (13—19th cent.) have been preserved, as well as the Old Cemetery. 14 other Jewish communities existed in other districts of the town (8 synagogues and 6 cemeteries have been preserved). — Old Cemetery in the centre of Prague, between the U starého hřbitova, 17. listopadu and Široká streets. F. in 1st half of 15th cent., oldest legible gravestone from 1439. Fragments of gravestones from mid--14th cent., transferred from older abolished cemetery. Burials until 1787. Gravestones of many prominent personalities, several tombs-sarcophagi (e. g. of the famous rabbi Yehuda Loew, d. 1609). A total of some 12,000 gravestones. The most valuable Jewish cemetery in Europe, of world significance. (p. 8, 58, 152, 172. 173)

PRAGUE-SMÍCHOV

Town district SW of centre. Jewish settlement from unknown date, documented from mid-18th cent. Jewish com-

munity f. in 1788, ceased to exist in World War II. 19th-
-cent. synagogue rebuilt in 1930—31 (now a storehouse).
— Old cemetery in U starého židovského hřbitova street,
on top of hill. F. probably in 1788, oldest legible gravestones from early 19th cent., burials until 1921. New cemetery in Liebknechtova street, f. in 1903, last burial in 1973.

(p. 61)

PRAGUE-ŽIŽKOV
Town district E of centre. Jewish settlement from unknown
date, Jewish community f. in 1888, ceased to exist in World
War II. Prayer hall was part of block of flats. — Two important cemeteries of the Prague Jewish community are
placed on the territory of Žižkov. Old cemetery in Fibichova
street f. in 1680 as burial place for plague victims. From
1787 (after cemetery in inner town was closed) it became
Prague's central cemetery, burials until 1890. In 1960,
a large part of cemetery abolished. Very valuable cemetery
with gravestones of many prominent personalities. New
cemetery in Nad vodovodem street, f. in 1890, the only
cemetery in Prague still in use. (p. 10, 60, 155)

PRUDICE
Village in S Bohemia, 10 km of district capital Tábor. Very
small Jewish settlement (one family for most of the time)
documented from early 18th cent. Existence of Jewish community based here documented only in 1st quarter of 18th
cent. In mid-19th cent. community based probably in the
village of Nemyšl (2 km E), ceased to exist probably before
1870. — Cemetery 0.5 km SW of Prudice, 0.5 km NE of Su-
doměřice railway station, on hill. F. at unknown date, existence documented in 1st quarter of 18th cent., oldest legible
gravestone from 1780, burials (of people from neighbouring
villages) until World War II. (p. 76)

PUCLICE (G: Putzlitz, Pustlitz)
Village in SW Bohemia, 14 km NNE of district capital Do-
mažlice. Jewish settlement from unknown date, documented
from 1st quarter of 18th cent. Jewish community f. at unknown date, existence documented from early 19th cent., offices transferred to the town of Staňkov (G. Markt Stankau,
3 km E) in 1892—93. Synagogue built in 1818, demolished
after 1975. — Cemetery 1 km SW of village green, at edge
of forest. F. allegedly in 18th cent., oldest preserved gravestones from 1st half of 19th cent., burials until World
War II. (p. 30)

RABÍ
Small town in SW Bohemia, district of Klatovy, 8 km NE of
Sušice. Records of Jewish settlement from late 15th cent.,
Jewish community probably existed then, documented

again from 1st quarter of 18th cent., abolished in late 19th
cent. Small synagogue adapted as private house. — Cemetery in W part of town, on NW slope of castle hill. F. at unknown date, documented from 1st quarter of 18th cent.,
preserved gravestones from 18th cent., last burial in early
20th cent. (p. 36)

RADENÍN
Village in S Bohemia, 13 km SE of district capital Tábor.
Records of Jewish settlement from 1st quarter of 17th cent.,
existence of Jewish community documented from 1st quar-

VELKÝ PĚČÍN

ter of 18th cent., abolished after 1921. Jewish quarter (ghetto); important from point of view of town-planning, with synagogue rebuilt as private house. — Valuable cemetery 800 m NE of village green, on hill. F. at unknown date, documented in 1st quarter of 18th cent., oldest legible gravestone from 1741, burials until World War II. (p. 96)

RADNICE
Town in W Bohemia, 13 km N of district capital Rokycany. Jewish settlement existed allegedly in 15th cent., document-

ed from 1st half of 16th cent. Existence of Jewish community documented from early 19th cent. (probably much older), abolished in 1935. Synagogue built in 1804 (now a workshop). — Cemetery 1.5 km E of town square, at edge of forest. F. at unknown date, oldest legible gravestone from 1763, burials until World War II. (p. 46)

RAKOVNÍK (G: Rakonitz)
District capital in C Bohemia. Records of Jewish settlement from 1st half of 15th cent. Jewish community f. probably in 17th cent., documented from 1st quarter of 18th cent., ceased to exist in World War II. 18th-cent. synagogue (now a concert hall). — Valuable cemetery at SE edge of town, in F. Diepolt street. F. in 1635, oldest legible gravestone from mid-17th cent., last burial in 1979. (p. 48)

ROKYTNICE V ORLICKÝCH HORÁCH (G: Rokitnitz in Adlergebirge)
Town in E Bohemia, 13 km E of district capital Rychnov nad Kněžnou. Records of Jewish settlement from 2nd half of 17th cent., existence of Jewish community documented from 1st quarter of 18th cent., abolished in 1893. Jewish street (19th-cent. synagogue demolished after World War II). — Cemetery 400 m SE of town square, at edge of forest. F. in 1718, oldest preserved gravestones from 1st quarter of 18th cent., burials probably until 1930s. Cemetery almost totally destroyed by the Nazis. (p. 119)

ROUDNICE NAD LABEM (G: Raudnitz a. d. Elbe)
Town in N Bohemia, 15 km SE of district capital Litoměřice. Jewish settlement from unknown date, documented from 1st half of 16th cent. Existence of Jewish community documented from late 16th cent., ceased to exist in World War II. Jewish street with mid-19th-cent. synagogue, rebuilt as boarding-house. — Very valuable old cemetery 800 m WNW of main square, Třebízského street. F. probably in 1613, oldest gravestone from 1611 (transferred from older, abolished cemetery), burials probably until 1890. New cemetery f. probably in 1890, used also after World War II, liquidated after 1985. (p. 52)

ROUSÍNOV (G: Neu-Raussnitz)
Town in C Moravia, district of Vyškov, 19 km E of centre of Brno. Jewish settlement probably from 15th cent., documented from mid-16th cent. Existence of Jewish community documented from late 16th cent., ceased to exist in World War II. Large Jewish quarter with synagogue built probably in late 16th cent., later rebuilt on several occasions (now chapels of the Czechoslovak Hussite Church, and Evangelical Church of Czech Brethren). — Very valuable cemetery

300 m S of town square, Skálova street. F. at unknown date, oldest legible gravestone from 1695, burials until World War II. (p. 138, 166)

ROŽMBERK NAD VLTAVOU (G: Rosenberg)

Small town in S Bohemia, 18 km SSE of district capital Český Krumlov. Jewish settlement allegedly from the Middle Ages, documented together with existence of Jewish community from 2nd half of 17th cent. Jewish community abolished in 1938 by the Nazis. 17th-cent. synagogue demolished after 1965. — Remains of old cemetery at S edge of town, adjacent to inner side of town fortifications. Allegedly of mediaeval origin, documented from 1st quarter of 18th cent., oldest preserved gravestones from mid-18th cent., burials probably until 1882. At the time of Nazi occupation and after World War II, cemetery badly damaged, but partly reconstructed later. — New cemetery 500 m NNW of town square. F. in 1883, last burial in 1950. (p. 88)

RYCHNOV NAD KNĚŽNOU (G: Reichenau)

District capital in E Bohemia. Records of Jewish settlement from 1st half of 16th cent., existence of Jewish community documented from early 17th cent., ceased to exist in World War II. Remains of Jewish street with late 18th-cent. synagogue (now empty, unused). — Valuable cemetery 600 m NW of town square, near road to the village of Lokot. F. in 1588 or 1616, oldest legible gravestone from 1690, burials until World War II. Memorial hall of victims of Nazism in the former mortuary or hearse shed. (p. 13, 119)

SLATINA

Village in SW Bohemia, district of Klatovy, 8 km NNE of Horažďovice. Jewish settlement from unknown date, documented from 17th cent. Existence of Jewish community documented from 1st half of 19th cent. (probably older), abolished in 1893. Remains of Jewish quarter, synagogue built in 1850 (now empty, unused). — Cemetery 1 km N of village, in forest. F. in 1723 by extension of older burial place. Burials from around 1668, oldest legible gravestone from 1755, last burial in 1937. (p. 40)

SLAVKOV U BRNA (G: Austerlitz)

Town in C Moravia, 16 km SW of district capital Vyškov. Jewish settlement existed probably in 2nd half of 13th cent., documented from 1st half of 14th cent. Existence of numerous Jewish community documented from 15th cent., ceased to exist in World War II. Remains of large Jewish quarter with synagogue built in 1858 (now a storehouse). — Valuable cemetery 1 km N of town square. F. in 1872, burials until World War II. Many gravestones transferred from older abolished cemetery (oldest legible from 1735). (p. 137)

SPÁLENÉ POŘÍČÍ (G: Brenn-Poritschen)

Small town in SW Bohemia, district of Plzeň-South, 14 km S of Rokycany. Records of Jewish settlement from 1st half of 17th cent., existence of Jewish community documented from mid-17th cent., abolished after 1921. Remains of Jewish quarter (synagogue built probably in 18th cent., demolished in 1946). — Cemetery 150 m NW of town square, Pražská street. F. at unknown date (allegedly 17th cent.), documented from 2nd half of 18th cent., oldest legible gravestone from 1801, burials probably until World War II. (p. 45)

STARÉ MĚSTO POD LANDŠTEJNEM (G: Altstadt)

Small town in S Bohemia, district of Jindřichův Hradec, 10 km ESE of Nová Bystřice. Jewish settlement from unknown date, documented from 1st third of 17th cent. Existence of Jewish community documented from mid-17th cent., abolished in 1893. Remains of Jewish quarter (synagogue built in 1st half of 19th cent., demolished around 1955). — Valuable cemetery 600 m N of town square, on rocky hill amidst meadows. Existence documented from early 17th cent., oldest legible gravestone from 1727, burials probably until 1930s. (p. 1, 91, 160)

ŠTĚNOVICE (G: Stienowitz)

Village in W Bohemia, district of Plzeň-South, 7 km SSE of centre of Plzeň. Records of Jewish settlement from early 17th cent., Jewish community f. probably in 2nd half of 18th cent., abolished after 1921. Synagogue built probably in 19th cent., demolished after 1950. — Cemetery at NE edge of village, on slope rising from stream. F. at unknown date, oldest legible gravestone from 1831, burials until 1930s. (p. 45)

STRÁŽ NAD NEŽÁRKOU (G: Platz)

Small town in S Bohemia, 11 km SW of district capital Jindřichův Hradec. Jewish settlement from unknown date, documented together with existence of Jewish community from 1st third of 19th cent. Jewish community (allegedly existing from 18th cent.) abolished probably in late 19th cent. Synagogue built probably in 1st half of 19th cent. (now a storehouse). — Cemetery 1.5 km W of town square, at edge of forest. F. at unknown date, existence documented from 1828, oldest legible gravestone from 1847, burials probably until 1930s. Before 1900, burials mostly of people from the community in Třeboň (G: Wittingau, 12 km SW). (p. 90)

STRÁŽNICE (G: Strassnitz)

Town in S Moravia, 14 km NEE of district capital Hodonín. Jewish community existed allegedly back in early 15th cent., ceased to exist at the time of Hussite wars. Jewish settlement documented again from late 15th cent., existence of Jewish community documented from 1st half of 17th cent., ceased to exist in World War II. Jewish quarter with synagogue of unknown age, rebuilt in 19th cent. (now a storehouse). — Valuable cemetery at NE edge of town, Sadová street, adjacent to chateau park. F. probably in 1st half of 17th cent., oldest legible gravestones from 1647, burials also after World War II. (p. 143)

STŘÍTEŽ (G: Schrittenz)

Village in SE Bohemia, 7 km NE of centre of district capital Jihlava. Records of Jewish settlement from 1st quarter of 18th cent. Existence of Jewish community not documented, probably never existed. — Cemetery 400 m SW of village centre, amidst fields. F. at unknown date, oldest legible gravestone from 1834, last burial in 1939. Small, largely devastated cemetery. (p. 123)

STUDENÝ

Village in SE Bohemia, district of Benešov, 20 km SE of Vlašim. Records of Jewish settlement from 1st half of 19th cent. (mostly one family). Jewish community never existed here. — Cemetery 700 m SE of village green, amidst fields. F. allegedly in 1700, oldest gravestones from 18th cent., burials until 1930s. The more recent ones mostly of people from the community in Křivsoudov (4 km NW), documented from mid-19th cent. (p. 67)

ŠVIHOV (G: Schwihau)

Town in SW Bohemia, 10 km N of district capital Klatovy. Records of Jewish settlement from 2nd half of 16th cent., existence of Jewish community documented from 2nd half of 17th cent., abolished probably in late 19th cent. Remains of Jewish street (18th-cent. synagogue demolished after 1960). — Very valuable old cemetery 600 m SEE of town square, before railway line. F. in 1644, oldest legible gravestone from the time of foundation, burials until last quarter of 19th cent. Remains of new cemetery f. probably in 1879, destroyed after World War II. (p. 5, 43)

SVOJŠÍN (G: Schweissing)

Village in W Bohemia, district of Tachov, 6 km NWW of Stříbro. Records of Jewish settlement from early 17th cent., existence of Jewish community documented from 2nd half of 17th cent., abolished in late 19th cent. Old synagogue built in 1st half of 19th cent., demolished after 1950, new synagogue built in 2nd half of 19th cent. rebuilt as private house. — Cemetery 3 km W of Svojšín, between the villages of Řebří and Ošelín, surrounded by forests. F. at unknown date, documented from 1660, oldest legible gravestone from 1743, burials until 1st third of 20th cent. Burials also of people from the community in Ošelín (G: Oschelin, 4 km W) and until 1900 from the community in Stříbro (G: Mies). (p. 151)

TACHOV (G: Tachau)

District capital in W Bohemia. Jewish settlement allegedly existed in 13th cent., documented from 15th cent. Jewish community allegedly existed in 13th cent., documented from mid-16th cent., abolished in 1938 by the Nazis. Remains of Jewish street (synagogue built in 1911—12 demolished by the Nazis). — Valuable old cemetery 450 m ESE of town square. F. at unknown date, documented in 1615, burials until 1933. Devastated by the Nazis, area reduced in 1968, after 1986 part of historical gravestones transferred to cemetery in Mariánské Lázně. New cemetery f. in 1933 (p. 28)

ŤELICE (G: Dölitschen)

Village in W Bohemia, district of Tachov, 13 km SW of Stříbro. Records of Jewish settlement from early 18th cent., Jewish community from 2nd half of 18th cent., abolished in late 19th cent. Wooden synagogue destroyed by fire in 1878. — Cemetery 800 m NNW of village centre, at edge of forest. F. probably in 18th cent., oldest legible gravestone from 1767, burials until 1930s. Burials also of people from the communities in Prostiboř (2 km NW) and Nedražice (G: Nedraschitz, 7 km E). (p. 31)

TOVAČOV (G: Tobitschau)

Town in C Moravia, 12 km SWW of district capital Přerov. Jewish settlement probably existed from 15th cent., documented from 1st half of 16th cent. Existence of Jewish community documented from early 17th cent. (probably older), abolished probably in early 20th cent., religious life continued until World War II. Jewish street (synagogue of unknown age demolished in 1956). — Valuable cemetery 300 m SW of town square. F. probably after mid-17th cent., last burial in 1941. Two gravestones (from 1614 and 1615) transferred from older abolished cemetery. 19th-cent. ceremonial hall with preserved furnishings. (p. 145)

TŘEBÍČ (G: Trebitsch)

District capital in SW Moravia. Records of Jewish settlement from 1st half of 15th cent., Jewish community from mid-16th cent., ceased to exist in World War II. Once among the most numerous Jewish communities in Moravia. Large, architecturally significant Jewish town, probably the best preserved ghetto in Europe. Old synagogue built in 17—19th cent. (now chapel of the Czechoslovak Hussite Church), new synagogue built in 18th cent. (now being adapted as concert hall). — Very valuable cemetery at N edge of town, Hrádek street. F. probably in 1st half of 17th cent., oldest legible gravestone from 1625, last burial in 1968. Ceremonial hall of 1903. (p. 126)

TŘEŠŤ (G: Triesch)
Town in SW Moravia, 14 km SW of district capital Jihlava. Jewish settlement probably back in 13th cent., documented from early 17th cent. Existence of Jewish community documented from 2nd half of 17th cent., ceased to exist in World War II. Jewish quarter with synagogue built probably in 1st half of 19th cent. (now chapel of the Czechoslovak Hussite Church). — Very valuable cemetery 1.5 km SSW of town square, near road to the village of Hodice. F. probably in 2nd half of 17th cent., oldest legible gravestone from 1705, burials until World War II. (p. 131)

TRHOVÝ ŠTĚPÁNOV (G: Markt-Stiepanau)
Small town in C Bohemia, district of Benešov, 8 km E of Vlašim. Jewish settlement allegedly from 15th cent., documented from 1st half of 17th cent. Existence of Jewish community documented from 1st quarter of 18th cent., abolished probably before World War I. — Valuable cemetery 600 m SW of town square, behind railway line. F. at unknown date, oldest preserved gravestone probably from 1st quarter of 18th cent., burials until World War II. (p. 67)

TURNOV
Town in N Bohemia, 12 km WSW of district capital Semily. Records of Jewish settlement from 1st half of 16th cent., existence of Jewish community documented from 1st half of 17th cent., ceased to exist in World War II. Remains of Jewish quarter with 18th-cent. synagogue (now a storehouse). — Valuable cemetery 0.5 km SW of town square, in street leading to railway whistle stop. F. probably in 1st quarter of 18th cent., burials also after World War II. Oldest gravestones from late 17th cent. (probably transferred from older abolished cemetery). (p. 115)

ÚBOČÍ (G: Amonsgrün)
Village in W Bohemia, 15 km SE of district capital Cheb. Jewish settlement from unknown date, documented from 1st half of 19th cent. Existence of Jewish community documented from 1st half of 19th cent., abolished in 1893. Remains of Jewish quarter (synagogue of unknown age demolished after

1960). — Cemetery 300 m SW of village, on slope rising from pond. F. at unknown date, oldest gravestones from 1st half of 19th cent., burials until early 20th cent., mostly of people from neighbouring town of Dolní Žandov (G: Unter-Sandau). (p. 24)

UHERSKÝ BROD (G: Ungarisch-Brod)
Town in SE Moravia, 14 km SEE of district capital Uherské Hradiště. Records of Jewish settlement from 15th cent., existence of Jewish community documented from early 17th

cent., ceased to exist in World War II. Once among the largest and most important Jewish communities in Moravia. 18th-cent. synagogue demolished after 1941, large Jewish quarter demolished after World War II. — Cemetery 0.5 km E of centre, in street leading to suburban district of Těšov. F. in 1870, still in use. Some 70 valuable gravestones (the oldest from 17th cent.) transferred from older cemetery destroyed at the time of Nazi occupation. Memorial to victims of Nazism in ceremonial hall. (p. 145)

ÚSOV (G: Mährisch-Aussee)
Small town in N Moravia, 18 km S of district capital Šumperk. Jewish settlement from unknown date, documented from 2nd half of 16th cent. Existence of Jewish community

documented from early 17th cent., abolished in 1938 by the Nazis. Jewish quarter with 18th-cent. synagogue (now chapel of the Evangelical Church of Czech Brethren). — Valuable cemetery at N edge of town, on hill. F. allegedly in 1st half of 17th cent., oldest legible gravestone from 1745, burials until World War II. 17th-cent. gravestones destroyed by the Nazis. (p. 146, 170)

VAMBERK (G: Wamberg)
Town in E Bohemia, 5 km SSE of district capital Rychnov nad Kněžnou. Records of Jewish settlement from 2nd half of 17th cent. Small Jewish community allegedly existed then (not documented). — Valuable cemetery 700 m N of town square. F. in last quarter of 17th century, oldest legible

gravestone from 1700, burials until World War II. Cemetery belonged to Jewish community based in Doudleby nad Orlicí (G: Daudleb a. d. Adler, 2 km SW). (p. 120)

VELKÁ BUKOVINA (G: Gross-Bok, Gross-Bocken)
Village in NE Bohemia, 13 km W of district capital Náchod. Jewish settlement from unknown date, allegedly from early 18th cent., documented together with Jewish community from 1st quarter of 19th cent. Community abolished probably in late 19th cent. Architecturally significant Jewish street (ghetto) with remains of synagogue built in 1st half of 19th cent. (demolished in early 20th cent.) — Valuable cemetery 0.5 km N of village, amidst fields. F. at unknown date, oldest gravestones from 18th cent., burials probably until late 19th cent. (p. 7, 119)

VELKÉ MEZIŘÍČÍ (G: Gross-Meseritsch)
Town in W Moravia, 24 km SSE of district capital Žďár nad Sázavou. Jewish settlement from unknown date, documented together with Jewish community from early 16th cent. Once a numerous community, ceased to exist in World War II. Jewish street with two synagogues. Old synagogue built in 16th cent. (now a storehouse), new synagogue built in 2nd half of 19th cent. (now a storehouse). — Valuable cemetery 300 m NE of town square, on slope. F. at unknown date, oldest legible gravestone from 1677, burials until World War II. (p. 132)

VELKÝ PĚČÍN (G: Gross-Pantschen)
Village in SW Moravia, district of Jindřichův Hradec, 6 km S of Telč. No Jewish community existed here. — Valuable cemetery 1.5 km NW of village, in forest. F. probably in 1st half of 17th cent., oldest legible gravestone from 1655, burials until 1879. From its foundation, cemetery belonged to Jewish community in Telč which founded a new cemetery in the town in 1879—80. (p. 132, 165)

VĚTRNÝ JENÍKOV (G: Windig-Jenikau)
Small town in SE Bohemia, 11 km NW of district capital Jihlava. Jewish settlement from unknown date, documented together with Jewish community from 1st quarter of 18th cent. Jewish community abolished probably around mid-19th cent. — Valuable cemetery 1 km SSW of town square. F. at unknown date, oldest legible gravestone from 1700, burials probably until late 19th cent. Burials also of people from the community in Úsobí (G: Pollerskirchen, 5 km NNE). (p. 125)

VLACHOVO BŘEZÍ (G: Wällisch-Birken)
Small town in S Bohemia, 8 km NW of district capital Pra-

chatice. Records of Jewish settlement from mid-17th cent., existence of Jewish community documented from 1st quarter of 18th cent., abolished before 1921. Remains of small Jewish quarter with small 18th-cent. wooden synagogue, adapted as private house. — Cemetery 400 m N of town square. F. probably in early 18th cent., oldest legible gravestone from 1729, burials until World War II. (p. 85)

VOLYNĚ (G: Wolin)
Town in S Bohemia, 10 km S of district capital Strakonice. Continuous Jewish settlement documented from 1st quarter of 16th cent. Jewish community existed probably back in 16th cent., documented from 1st quarter of 18th cent., ceased to exist in World War II. Remains of Jewish street with synagogue built in 1st half of 19th cent. (now a cinema). — Valuable cemetery 400 m NW of town square. F. probably in 17th cent., oldest legible gravestone from 1689, burials until World War II. (p. 83)

VOTICE (G: Wotitz)
Town in C Bohemia, 16 km SSW of district capital Benešov. Jewish settlement from unknown date, documented together with Jewish community from 1st half of 16th cent. Community ceased to exist in World War II. Remains of ghetto (18th-cent. synagogue demolished in 1950). — Valuable cemetery 0.5 km E of town square. F. at unknown date, documented from 1st half of 16th cent., oldest legible gravestone from 1705, last burial in 1962. (p. 76)

ZÁJEZDEC (G: Sajestetz)
Village in E Bohemia, 10 km SEE of district capital Chrudim. Jewish settlement from unknown date, documented together with Jewish community from 1st quarter of 18th cent. Jewish community abolished before 1896. Synagogue built probably in 18th cent., demolished in 1925. — Cemetery at N edge of village. F. at unknown date, oldest legible gravestone from 1789, burials (also of people from the town Chrast) probably until 1st third of 20th cent. (p. 106)

ŽAMBERK (G: Senftenberg)
Town in E Bohemia, 13 km NNE of district capital Ústí nad Orlicí. Existence of Jewish settlement and Jewish community documented from mid-17th cent., community ceased to exist in World War II. Jewish street with early 19th-cent. synagogue, completely rebuilt in mid-20th cent. (now chapel used by four Christian churches). — Valuable cemetery 400 m W of town square. F. probably in 17th cent., oldest legible gravestone from 1731, burials until World War II. Ceremonial hall of 1932. (p. 121)

Jiří Fiedler

172

OLD BOHEMIAN AND MORAVIAN JEWISH CEMETERIES

Petr Ehl, Arno Pařík, Jiří Fiedler

Translation © 1991 by
Greta Sylvia Matoušková and Zoja Joachimová.
Cover, binding and layout by Aleš Krejča.
First published 1991 by Paseka Prague
as its 13th publication.
Editor: Jiří Pondělíček.
Technical editor: Jarmila Mašková.
Printed by Svoboda, a. s., Praha
Writing-type Digi Baskerville
59-603-91

ISBN 80-85192-12-8

PRAHA-JOSEFOV